INCREDIBLE BOSSES

The challenge of managing people for incredible results

David Freemantle

McGRAW-HILL BOOK COMPANY

London · New York · St Louis · San Francisco · Auckland
Bogotá · Caracas · Hamburg · Lisbon · Madrid · Mexico · Milan
Montreal · New Delhi · Panama · Paris · San Juan · São Paulo
Singapore · Sydney · Tokyo · Toronto.

Dedication

To my loved ones:

Mechi
Ruth-Elena and Linnet
Tom and Kate
Mum and Dad

Published by
McGRAW-HILL Book Company Europe
Shoppenhangers Road, Maidenhead, Berkshire, SL6 2QL, England
Telephone 0628 23432
Fax 0628 770224

British Library Cataloguing in Publication Data
Freemantle, David.
  Incredible Bosses: Challenge of Managing
  People for Incredible Results. – New ed
  I. Title
  658.3

  ISBN 0—07—707689—3 SC
  ISBN 0—07—707314—2 HC

Library of Congress Cataloging-in-Publication Data
Freemantle, David.
  Incredible bosses: the challenge of managing people for
  incredible results / David Freemantle.
  p.   cm.
  ISBN 0—07—707689—3 SC
  ISBN 0—07—707314—2 HC
  1. Personnel management.   I. Title.
  [HF5549.F695   1992]
  658.3—dc20   92–4340
                                                  CIP

1234 B&S 9432

Typeset by Wyvern Typesetting Limited, Bristol
Printed and bound in Great Britain by Billing & Sons Ltd, Worcester

Contents

Foreword   ix
Acknowledgements   xi
Introduction   xiii

Part 1   CONCEPTS   1

1   Managerial competence   3
2   Integrity   7
3   Credibility   9

Part 2   PHILOSOPHY

1   Deep-thinking   15
2   Communication vs. miscommunication   17
3   Beliefs   24
4   Values   27
5   Vision   30
6   Standards   33
7   Openness   35
8   Truth and honesty   38
9   Trust   42
10   Mutual respect   46
11   Caring   49
12   Practising what you preach   51
13   Consultation: the reality vs. the myth   54
14   The dangers of cosmetic training   57
15   Courage of convictions   61
16   Recognizing one's own deficiencies   65

Contents

Part 3   PSYCHOLOGY   67

1   Emotional management   69
2   The art of listening and valuing   71
3   Perception and self-deception   74
4   Inner dignity and intrinsic worth   78
5   Hidden agendas and ulterior motivations   81
6   From frustration to inspiration   84
7   Converting weaknesses to strengths   87
8   The uncertainty factor   90
9   Selfish needs   92
10   Indirect signals   95
11   Stereotyping   97
12   Subjective assessment   99
13   Personality clashes   102
14   Passive resistance   104
15   Fear of owning up   107
16   Protection mechanisms   110
17   Problem avoidance   113
18   Rationalization   117
19   Prejudice: the invidious management disease   120
20   Closed minds   123
21   Sycophancy   127
22   Management by intimidation   131
23   Rituals   135
24   Totem poles   137
25   Taboos   139
26   The denigration syndrome   141
27   Inner circles, clans, cliques and clubs   144
28   Managerial helplessness   147

Part 4   INTEGRITY GAPS   151

1   Erosion of integrity   153
2   Hypocrisy   156
3   Deceiving the public   159
4   Image manipulation   161

5	Advertising deceptions	163
6	Erosion of media integrity	165
7	Customer insensitivity	167
8	Corporate talk and employee deception	170
9	Short-term expediency	175
10	Double-standards	178
11	Alarmism	181
12	Cover-ups	184
13	Guesswork	187
14	Negotiating games	189
15	'I hear what you say'	192
16	Papering over the cracks	194
17	Carrot pay	199
18	Self-entertainment	201
19	Mindless memos	203
20	Information games	206
21	Internal politics	209
22	Patronage	211
23	Disbelieving bosses	213
Part 5	TEN STEPS	217
Step 1	Self-starting	219
Step 2	Honesty rating	221
Step 3	Confirmation of beliefs and values	223
Step 4	Establishing a vision of success	228
Step 5	Determining levels of integrity	231
Step 6	Resolving conflicts	234
Step 7	Let employees be themselves	236
Step 8	Check your conscience	239
Step 9	Ensure consistency	241
Step 10	Finding time to think	243

Foreword

Over the last few years I have worked with hundreds of organizations in a variety of industries including transportation, retail, hotels, financial services, manufacturing, local government and other public services. Literally thousands of managers have participated intensively in my training programmes, workshops, seminars and consultations. Much of this book is drawn from such participation as well as from my previous experience in senior management in a number of organizations.

In fact I keep careful notes of what people say to me, and what they say is often incredible! Throughout this book I have taken the liberty of quoting from these notes as illustrations. Sad to say, the majority are about incredibly bad bosses. They represent the hidden but horrible reality of modern management practice. A minority are about those incredibly rare good bosses, whom I prefer to call superbosses.

It is tempting in all this to disclose identities, job titles and names of organizations. This I know would add credibility and further colour to the text. After careful reflection I have decided against this, not wishing to embarrass any of the many managers who have indirectly contributed to this book. Their open and honest comments about their incredible bosses have helped me immeasurably in developing my theme. I thank them all.

Acknowledgements

I am deeply indebted to Roger Horton for all his support and the innumerable hours he put in to helping me conceptualize the idea for INCREDIBLE BOSSES and furthermore his valuable advice on how my first draft could be extensively improved.

I am also extremely grateful to my wife Mechi for all the hard work she put in to helping me revise the final version.

Introduction

The key is *credibility* as a reflection of *integrity*. The worst bosses lose it while the very best manage to achieve it.

Incredibly, the day I began writing this book the Prime Minister, Mrs Thatcher, was accused in Parliament by Neil Kinnock, Leader of the Opposition, of being a cheat. He later withdrew the remark. Whom do you believe?

The same day a newspaper reported a row over 'TV Lies' in the run up to the American presidential election. Both Dukakis and Bush were accusing each other of lying. Who was credible?

Also reported in the newspaper that day was progress on the case of an international financier who, it was alleged, had diverted his clients' money in offshore funds into his own private ventures. Who would credit a top boss doing such a thing?

Another story that day related to a brain-damaged girl receiving an award for damages approaching a million pounds following a hospital accident seven years earlier. It had taken the authorities five years to admit liability. It's just incredible that they didn't own up in the first place.

During one short day, then, there were four newspaper reports relating to lapses in credibility and integrity. In fact, you can find incredible reports about mismanagement and poor leadership every day in the newspapers, for example stories about water boards trying a cover-up over a poisoned river, about an accountant who is sacked for telling the truth to the tax people, about garages who cheat motorists in failing to carry out services properly, about senior police officers who maliciously blame hooligans for a disaster resulting from inadequate policing. Then there is the Guinness affair and insider-dealing scandals in the City.

Lapses in credibility and integrity can frequently lead to disaster. The inquiry judge on a major ferry disaster in March 1987 spoke of underlying cardinal faults by management leading to the loss of 188 lives, of shore management taking little notice of its captains, of the ferry firm's disease of sloppiness. Not listening to the experts nor believing them is a common lapse of integrity displayed by bosses who are incredibly incompetent. The inquiry report on an underground station disaster in November 1987 revealed senior management's 'blind-spot' about safety leading to a loss of 32 lives. Placing a higher value on money than on safety (or people) is another common lapse of integrity displayed by incredibly bad bosses.

Lapses in credibility and integrity hit the headlines frequently. Yet these are only the tip of the iceberg. Less blatant lapses are common occurrences in many organizations where stories abound about unbelievable managers who never do what they say, or do something different, or deny having said what they said, or just tell lies. Diminishing management credibility is endemic in the modern commercial world and leads to low morale, distrust, poor performance and ultimately failure.

Conversely those who are often most credible rarely get accredited for it. In the long term it is these people who achieve the most. The *incredibly good bosses* achieve long-term commercial success by developing open, honest and trusting relationships with their customers, employees and suppliers. Such relationships are based on the highest levels of mutual belief and integrity.

This book is far from being a moral tract. Nor is it a regurgitation of lessons you'd normally be taught at business school. Its aim is to explore what I believe is a fundamental and underlying principle of long-term business success.

Unbelievably that principle is *credibility* through the establishment of mutual belief and integrity. In application that principle is as elusive a management goal as any. Credibility and integrity are personal qualities which most managers, if they ever gave

'When the Managing Director joined a couple of years ago he called all the managers together on the first day. He told us he believed in an open and honest style of management and that's what he wanted to introduce into the company. Cynics like me had heard it all before and didn't really believe him. His predecessor was always saying things like that but was only honest when it suited him.

'Two years later I can honestly say that we have here a more open and honest style of management than I've ever come across in any other company. It reaches down to all levels of employees. For example, the day after each monthly board meeting the 80 managers in the company are invited to attend a briefing session about what went on at the board. The briefing is always comprehensive and frank, very little is withheld from us. Our questions are invariably answered honestly and genuinely. We all feel we know what's going on, we feel involved.

'With the board being so open and honest in this way it's so much easier to be open and honest with our people down the line, something I personally was unable to do with the previous regime.'

much thought to the matter, would say they had, but which for all practical purposes, they frequently lack.

Fires spread through underground systems, passenger ferries sink and organizations fail through lapses in integrity. The bosses don't believe their people and their people don't believe their bosses. Incredible! These lapses are mostly non-criminal and due to an unthinking approach to management leading to behaviours which generate distrust and disbelief. Such managers become *unbelievable*.

Conversely, long-term business success can only be achieved, in my view, when the values of total trust, openness and honesty are pursued throughout an organization and beyond towards its employees, customers, suppliers and for that matter all external contacts.

There are deep and dark subconscious forces within most organizations which mitigate against the pursuit of integrity and thus credibility, forces which can eventually lead to the destruction of that organization and the jobs of its people. These forces derive from the uncontrolled growth of informal but semi-corrupt value systems which in turn lead to the passive toleration by the majority of deviant behaviours.

Nothing is perfect and absolute integrity and credibility can never be achieved. However the pursuit of perfection, of integrity and of being believed by the people around you is as much an important goal in business as it is in everyday life. Such a pursuit requires a frequent re-appraisal of organization and individual value-systems together with the elimination or at least acceptance of weaknesses and imperfections thrown up by such an appraisal. Truth is of the essence in this re-appraisal process and the establishment of belief. Yet truth for many people is an unpalatable commodity, especially when focussed upon an organization's and an individual's weaknesses, imperfections and 'semi-corrupt' values.

Furthermore, truth is an intangible commodity, enshrouded by perceptions, opinions, prejudices, historical biases as well as distinct lapses in objective judgement. Truth is something 'we' believe we have and others don't. But that's not the truth. The real truth about organization and individual inadequacy is often denied in favour of a deceptive but more comfortable 'simulated' truth divorced from a reality seen by all but the decision-maker.

'Simulated credibility', for example, manifested by unfulfilled bureaucratic assertions such as you find in company reports ('our people are our greatest asset' or 'much emphasis is placed on employee communications') can have a highly damaging impact on an organization, destroying belief and creating incredibly bad bosses. These assertions ('simulated truths') while well-intended are frequently at odds with the everyday experience of people in the company and thus engender disbelief and cynicism.

It takes a courageous person to own up to his or her own weaknesses, inadequacies and imperfections, especially if they have been substantially reflected in the historical development of the organization and what it stands for today. The person who builds and develops a company over 20 years will be the last person to admit failure when it goes bankrupt. So unpalatable are the unpleasant truths of life that they are often projected away from the individual on to the organization and then on outwards to external forces for blame.

Such a lack of integrity often exists in people perceived as having the highest level of it. In the examples given in the first two paragraphs of this Introduction, who was lacking in integrity? Who was believable?

Modern management practice advocates 'stressing the positive and building on strengths' rather than exposing and eliminating weaknesses. It is the province of politics to do the latter.

Yet a weakness is a weakness. One cannot escape that truth. No one is perfect. One cannot escape that truth either. The skill of the manager is 'how' to identify a weakness and then 'how' to deal with it. The answer is not to avoid the weakness by stressing the positive, for that would lead to distorted perceptions and further lapses of credibility. Any individual who genuinely desires to improve will welcome 'positive' identification of weaknesses and constructive advice on their elimination. The skill, and it is a rare management skill, is how to achieve this improvement process without loss of face, loss of inner dignity or, more tangibly, loss of pay, status, standing and promotion prospects. The skill can only be practised when there is a mutual relationship based on credibility and integrity. If the organization value system supports openness, honesty and the development of trust between all employees then that skill will come relatively easy. Sadly in most organizations this is not the case.

The pursuit of credibility and integrity is not easy, in fact it is an elusive goal. However in my view it is essential for long-term

---

'They changed the leave arrangements for all staff. I manage a department of over a hundred people. I only found out when one of the staff came up to me and said she'd heard something from one of the shop-stewards about changing the leave arrangements. I knew nothing about it and as usual I felt a right fool, this sort of thing really undermines your credibility as a boss. But it's the practice here, managers only find out things through the back door.'

---

business success. Throughout this book you will be challenged constantly on your own levels of credibility and integrity and therefore the degree to which you are an incredible boss.

Part 1 provides an examination of the three key inter-related *concepts* upon which the thesis of this book is based. This is that managerial competence (and thus long-term success) is a function of integrity and credibility.

In Part 2 the *underlying philosophy* necessary for achieving integrity is considered. There are also a large number of *psychological factors* which have a major impact on competence and thus credibility. These are explored in Part 3.

Where low integrity exists in an organization a large number of 'integrity gaps' tend to appear. These lead to demotivation and consequently incompetence and failure. Part 4 identifies a number of these gaps.

Finally in Part 5 *ten key steps* to becoming an incredibly good boss are recommended.

Like my previous two books, *Superboss* and *Profitboss* this book can either be read straight through or on a 'dip-in' *section-a-day* basis.

'When I was a junior I had this great boss who would actually listen to me. I found that if I had a good point to make I could actually influence him, that he'd actually take on board my ideas, my advice and act accordingly.

'It was an important lesson I learnt very early in my management career. I go out of my way now to listen to all my people, including the most junior. In fact it's they who come up with some of the best ideas. I mean it was the receptionist's idea to serve coffee in reception. Not a revolutionary idea but nobody in this organization had thought about it before her!'

When I first tried to get this book published (using the title *Integrity*) one publisher wrote back to me rejecting it, saying that 'he had no faith in managers wishing to conduct themselves with greater integrity'. Another wrote 'the subject – integrity – ought to be of great interest to business readers, but my experience tells me that they rarely buy what they ought to'. My experience over recent years indicates that a large majority of executives are keen to establish a high degree of credibility by achieving high standards of integrity. They believe like me that commercial success and profit in the long term are best derived from such principles and pursuits. This book is intended to help such executives.

Part 1

CONCEPTS

The thesis upon which this book is based is that managerial competence and thus success derives from integrity and credibility.

●

In this part of the book each of these three inter-related concepts will be considered.

1

Managerial competence

'It is always someone else who is incompetent.'

I meet few incompetent managers. In fact I've never met one who's admitted being incompetent. It's always someone else.

Organizations develop sophisticated performance measurement schemes to identify those others who are incompetent.

'But it's not me. I'm competent. I work very hard for this organization. I've always done my best for it. It's just that my contribution is not recognized and valued by my boss.'

Usually when managers perceived as incompetent are fired you find that they have reasons other than incompetence for being removed from their jobs. 'My face didn't fit.' 'I couldn't get on with my new boss.' 'My problem was I spoke up, told the truth. They didn't like that. I got fired.'

- Is telling the truth incompetence?

- Is a personality clash with the boss incompetence?

- Is incompatibility with the team incompetence?

Yet managerial incompetence manifestly does exist. A company that goes out of business must have, by definition, incompetent managers. The low morale prevalent in many organizations is most often a product of managerial incompetence.

It is the very managers who create low morale through a blatant disregard for their people that consider themselves competent. Their own failures they see as due to others' incompetence.

Incredibly it is always someone else.

Bad bosses, being experts in other people's incompetence, never question their own competence.

Conversely good bosses are reluctant to attribute failure to others, preferring to challenge their own inadequacies before rushing into judgement.

Managerial competence and incompetence is a function of (but not equal to) credibility. Regrettably, a lack of credibility in the eyes of the decision-maker is often regarded as incompetence.

If one defines competence as *'achieving the required results'* and credibility (in the context of performance) as a *'belief by others that the required results have been achieved with integrity'*, then the incredibly good bosses score high (10/10) on the matrix shown in Figure 1 while incredibly poor bosses score low (0/0).

Competence therefore cannot be dissociated from credibility (or for that matter integrity). It is quite possible for an incompetent person (10/0) to stay in a job because he or she has a high degree of credibility in the eyes of his or her boss. Conversely it is quite possible for a very competent person (0/10) to get fired because of a lack of credibility in the eyes of his or her boss.

The credibility/competence gap arises for a number of reasons:

1. With few exceptions the measurement of individual competence is unbelievably difficult and often highly suspect.

   Ideally individual results should be quantifiable if not qualifiable. However such results can be distorted in team situations where individuals are dependent on others. The same applies when managers' freedoms are restricted by the machinations of large organizations. External factors also condition the end result.

   Superbosses rise above organization machinations and constraining external factors to achieve exceptionally good results. These are for all to see. But it is wrong to deduce, by comparison, that all other bosses are incompetent.

   Is it incompetent to accept organization decisions which

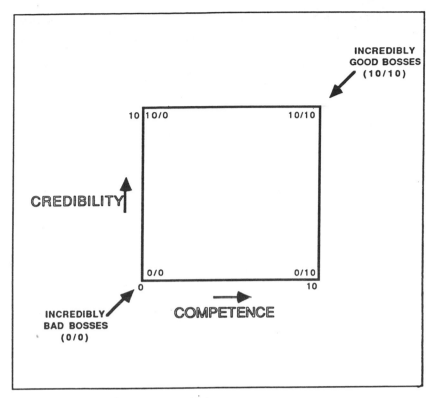

Figure 1 Credibility/competence matrix

inhibit you from achieving the goals the organization sets you? Or is it incompetent to challenge corporate decisions at the risk of alienating your boss and those more senior in the hierarchy?

2. Subjectivity reigns in the assessment of competence despite the emphasis placed on performance assessment techniques. Such techniques often tend to become illusory, proferring no more than a cosmetic of objectivity while managers manipulate the system to record subjective views objectively.

The perception of competence is enhanced if the person being assessed is credible in the eyes of the boss (or the assessor). Factors enhancing credibility often have little to do with competence – for example, a likeable personality, a willing attitude, an acquiescent 'yes-boss' subservience. Conversely, factors diminishing credibility might well be due to enhanced competence – for example, contravening a nonsensical regulation to achieve an important result for the organization.

3. Divergent values and beliefs have a major impact on credibility but not necessarily on competence. Ethically one should not discriminate against a competent individual who does not subscribe to the same values and beliefs as the boss. In practice however a dissident member of the team tends to be ostracized and consequently labelled 'incompetent' no matter how competent in the achievement of results.

In the following two chapters the inter-related concepts of integrity and credibility are explored.

2

Integrity

'Integrity is an ideal state'

Integrity is a totality, a wholeness. It is when every single person in the organization subscribes to its values and behaves in a way consistent with them.

Furthermore it is when every single person behaves in a way consistent with his or her own values – for example, values of honesty, openness, trust and caring. It is when an organization's support systems derive from and comply consistently with the culture of the organization as well as the professed values of its leaders.

It is when managers say what they mean and mean what they say. It is when managers' actions are totally consistent with their words and their words totally consistent with their individual as well as organization's beliefs.

'I'm a very creative person and used to have a lot of scope before they brought in this new team at the top. The only creative thing I do now is invent names for them.

'For example we have "Mirror Management" (I'll look into that), or "Lozenge Management" (We'll suck it and see) or "Boomerang Management" (I'll come back to you), or "Calendar Management' (Give us a month) or "Ear-Muffin Management" (I hear what you say).

'The trouble is it's all words, never any action. They never look into things, they never suck it and see, they never come back to us, they are forever procrastinating and, of course, they don't really listen.'

Integrity is when customers share the same perception of an organization's values as its employees and leaders. It is when there is a totality of honesty, openness and respect among all those associated with the organization, whether they be suppliers, external contacts, customers, staff or senior executives.

Integrity is rarely achieved and if so only temporarily. Few managers even attempt to achieve it. Those that do, in my view, are those that achieve the greatest long-term commercial success.

> 'I had this great idea to save the company some money. I presented it to our management committee. "Yes, Elizabeth," they said, "that's great, just what we want, go ahead and implement it." It was even in the minutes of that month's committee. Yet when I tried to get some time with the various managers on the committee whose help I needed to introduce the idea I just met a brick wall. Most were too busy to see me. One or two promised they would get things done on my behalf, but nothing happened. It was all lip-service. They appease you with fine words but never do anything really to support you.'

Integrity is an ideal state. However there is nothing wrong with idealism, especially if the pursuit of the ideal has a positive impact on what you set out to achieve, as a manager, today. Credibility is reflection of the degree of integrity a person has in achieving the required results. This will be considered in the next chapter.

Experience shows that both short-term and long-term business success does in fact derive from the pursuit of the integrity ideal.

3

Credibility

'Credibility is a reflection of a boss's integrity. It is one of the vital factors in the success or failure of management.'

At one end of the spectrum certain bosses achieve spectacular successes that defy belief, often going against organization convention, defying authority and displaying a degree of initiative and innovation which lesser mortals thought impossible. Such incredible bosses inevitably inspire and motivate their people to sustain high levels of performance. Such bosses achieve a high degree of credibility.

At the other end of the spectrum certain bosses drag their organizations towards disaster, often behaving in ways that defy common sense and are contrary to what most sensible people think wise. These incredibly bad bosses lose all credibility.

While credibility derives from personal success, this success in turn derives from the degree of integrity shown by managers in relating their deeds to their words and beliefs.

Between the extremes of incredible success and incredible failure is a spectrum of credibility and integrity along which most managers move.

What many managers fail to realize is that every small piece of behaviour and every word they utter influences their own credibility (as a reflection of integrity) in the eyes of others.

If a manager's behaviour and words are inconsistent with expressed organization values, or more importantly with those of the

Be totally honest with yourself and try to assess your own position across the following spectrum:

LOW ⟵	⟶ HIGH
CREDIBILITY	CREDIBILITY
LOW INTEGRITY	**HIGH INTEGRITY**
Inconsistent decisions	Consistent decisions
Indecisive	Decisive
Poor listener	Good listener
Poor/slow grasp of complex situations	Good/quick grasp of complex situations
Subservient	Prepared to challenge
Arrogant	Humble
Closed	Open
Not trusted	Trusted
Intolerant	Tolerant
Defensive	Prepared to admit mistakes
Aggressive	Controlled
Confused set of values/beliefs	Clear and strong set of values/beliefs
Lacks courage	Courageous
Insensitive	Sensitive
Selfish	Caring
Dismissive	Respectful
Manipulative	Straight
Devious	Principled
Game–player	Results–oriented
Unsupportive	Supportive
Dishonest	Honest
Reluctant to change	Innovative
Blows with the wind	Self-directed
Controlled by destiny	Controls own destiny
Discourteous	Courteous
Thinks money	Thinks people
Covers up	Owns up

How did you rate yourself? A high rating is only valid if you have the confidence to repeat the exercise with your team and they come up with the same answer!

boss, then the credibility of that manager will diminish. Furthermore, if such behaviour and words are inconsistent with the person's own previously expressed values and beliefs then credibility will be diminished further. There will be an erosion of integrity.

It is even more complex than that, because some people continually diminish their own credibility in the process of striving to enhance it. The 'yes-minister' syndrome is exactly that. People act out roles divorced from their own self in order to appease others. Such appeasement might achieve short-term credibility but in the long term their credibility will be diminished, the 'yes-person' being perceived as false, a hypocrite or a charlatan.

Achieving credibility is therefore a complex process. To strive for it too much can lead to incompetence while to ignore it can also result in incompetence. In the first case the person seeks to be credible in the eyes of everyone. Being 'all things to all people' is impossible. The sad fact of life is that one cannot please all the people all the time. What is credible to one person is incredible to another. Perception therefore plays a major role in establishing credibility. This will be covered in a later chapter.

In the second case (of the person who doesn't worry about credibility) there is a danger that he or she does their own thing regardless of others. The resulting alienation can diminish such a person's credibility and therefore competence in achieving the required result.

The incredibly good bosses have the solution. It is a simple solution to a complex problem. They become credible to themselves. They establish their own beliefs as well as believe in themselves. They are bosses who have learned from their everyday working experience, who have challenged their own perceptions and understandings and over a period of years established a personal set of values and beliefs. They are people who have discovered their own personal strengths, weaknesses, ambitions, aspirations, likes and dislikes, and who can be open and honest about them. Such openness and honesty gives them integrity and credibility; it makes them incredibly good bosses. People find them believable, believing in them for what they are. Incredibly bad bosses are unbelievable because they try to make themselves out to be what they are not. They lack integrity and therefore credibility.

If you haven't really discovered yourself for what you are, if you haven't really worked through and developed your own beliefs, values and philosophy of management, then the probability is that you will try to imitate others, or react by the seat of your pants. You will act out a role and the more roles you act out the more your credibility will be reduced with a consequential negative impact on integrity and competence.

'In my early days I did a deal with a customer which backfired on me. It cost the company a lot of money. The company mounted an investigation. I had a new boss then. She stood by me all the while. She fought my corner, supported me and helped me through an incredibly difficult patch. She was the best boss I ever had. I learnt a lot from her.'

Part 2

PHILOSOPHY

To achieve high levels of managerial competence, incredibly successful bosses evolve a clear philosophy of management. It forms the foundation upon which they build success. It forms the basis of the decisions they make on a day-by-day basis.

●

Integrity is the coherence between those decisions and that philosophy and is thus reflected in their credibility.

●

In the following part of the book various aspects of that philosophy are considered. It is essentially a pragmatic philosophy.

1

Deep-thinking

'Integrity and credibility and thereby management success cannot be sustained without time for some deep-thinking.'

An intrinsic part of the superboss's philosophy of management is to create time for deep-thinking.

Deep-thinking requires a refusal to accept ideas, opinions, statements, presentations at face value, whether they be yours or those of others. Deep-thinking is the process of exploring and challenging every conceivable thought and thereby discovering inconceivable thoughts. It is the process of probing in depth the boundaries of your own understanding and knowledge. It is essentially a learning process, learning about yourself – about how your own actions relate to your words and beliefs. It is a matter of the constant re-evaluation of those beliefs, constant criticisms of your words and actions.

An automatic response to a request is not deep-thinking. A defensive reaction to a criticism is not deep-thinking. Articulating the first thought that comes into your head is not deep-thinking.

Deep-thinking requires immense time. We cannot discover what we are or where we should be going without deep-thinking.

Mad managers rush around reacting to events and at best give five seconds' worth of thought to important decisions. That's why they are mad. They never have time to listen – to themselves, let alone others. They never learn.

Wise managers, the very best, devote time to thinking about the way they lead, about how to succeed, about how to achieve the best. By investing time to examine and challenge themselves they become even wiser.

Sitting in the bath, going for long walks, taking holidays, travelling in trains and planes might provide golden opportunities for deep-thinking. They should not be missed, in fact such opportunities should be created.

However deep-thinking is not necessarily a solitary occupation. In a comfortable environment, without pressure, the interaction within a team, facilitated by an excellent leader or chairperson, can provide a perfect opportunity for deep-thinking. Team members have an immense capability of exploring and challenging each others' thoughts, of sparking new creative ideas from one another in the quest for discovering new routes for even greater success.

Deep-thinking requires integrity, recreates integrity. The more you reach into yourself (and into the team) the more you are forced to be open and honest about what's inside. The route to the truth is inescapable if you think deeply enough about it. The surface behaviours, delusions, protection mechanisms, impressive postures and acting-out roles can be swept aside the more you think about what you (and the team) are and how you relate to the world – and how the world relates to you.

The world does not relate to you merely through a process of surface interactions based on surface perceptions. That is a deception. The world relates to you, and you to it, in a way that is not always immediately obvious. You have to dig deeply below the surface to discover the reality. The reality, once discovered, might prove exceptionally painful to accept. But once you've accepted it, it will give you immense strength. It is the source of all management integrity and credibility.

Remember, the truth does not just appear on the surface. One has to dig deep to explore what's really below, and that requires time for some in-depth thinking – by yourself and with your team.

2

Communication vs. miscommunication

'Miscommunication is the germ which diminishes the credibility of many bosses.'

> 'The union representatives are always up on the seventh floor chatting to the directors. We never get invited up. The union knows more of what's going on in the company than we senior managers.'

To perform effectively, employees need to feel that their individual and team contributions are appreciated, that their ideas for future success are considered and understood. They need to get feedback on corporate as well as departmental progress. They need to understand the real problems facing the organization as well as their own department. They need to know what is on the mind of their boss, what he or she is thinking about them, about their progress or lack of it. They need feedback on how they can improve their own performance. They need an opportunity to air their grievances and concerns, their aspirations and hopes, their own thoughts. They need to feel that their boss is interested in them, is prepared to help them develop their careers. They need sensitive handling when things go wrong at home, when they feel bad at work – as most people occasionally do. They need to share in the excitement of success.

They need effective communications.

Regrettably much communication nowadays is ineffective. Formalized briefing groups, bland company newspapers, exhortatory videos and whistle-stop 'walk-the-patch' visits from senior executives rarely meet the communication needs of employees.

> 'These directors waste their time walking about. It's the latest fashion, that's why they do it. If you ask them a question all you get is the "stock answer" you've heard a thousand times before. If you press the point they become dismissive and try to change the topic.'

Bosses who are too rushed to spend time with their teams, who are never available at critical moments, who don't involve people in where the department or company is going, who rarely report back on progress, who are reluctant to confide in their staff are bosses who rarely meet the communication needs of employees. An organization that frowns upon time spent off-job in communications and training, that creates an attitude that 'time spent talking' (or even worse listening) is wasted, is an organization that undervalues communication. Conversely an organization in which no decision can be made without everyone having their say is an organization that doesn't understand effective communications.

All are instances of management miscommunication, a disease that is endemic in many organizations today.

> 'I read about it in the *Evening Standard*. We'd secured that all important defence contract. Apparently my boss had found out in the morning but he'd been too busy to tell us. So much for excellent communication in this company!'

While most senior executives agree on the importance of effective employee communications many pay mere lip-service to it. The main reasons for this superficial approach are:

1. Managers don't fully understand the importance of communication.

2. Managers tend to undervalue it, placing higher priorities on urgent professional, technical or commercial activities.

3. They find it a painful process having to justify decisions to their people.

4. People are themselves difficult, often throwing up objections and complaints. Many managers prefer to avoid this by dismissing their people as 'belly-achers'.

5. Managers find it difficult to follow through on all the issues that are raised with them.

6. Managers perceive that their employees cannot be trusted with 'confidential' information.

7. Managers fear adverse reactions from their employees if they are told the truth on controversial subjects.

8. Managers have not been fully trained in employee communications and fail to differentiate between passing information down, listening, consulting, involving and participating, negotiation, exhortation. They have not thought through whether it's more effective to meet face-to-face, telephone or write in order to communicate.

> 'They expect 120 per cent all the time. It's all they are interested in. But they don't communicate, they don't seem to care about us. There are rumours of reorganization. I haven't the faintest idea whether there will be a job for me soon. I've given my best but I don't think they know. All they are interested in is the bottom line. It's all take as far as they're concerned, but there's no give. I'm just fed up with it.'

To avoid these problems managers miscommunicate under pretence of effective communications. They set up formalized communication processes to by-pass the painful face-to-face sessions really required down the line. Information is censored and then translated by 'experts' into bland exhortatory generalizations by way of notices, newsletters, videos and stand-up presentations. Opportunities for challenge are reduced to a minimum, the prospect of challenge from below being perceived as a dissident threat as opposed to a learning opportunity.

A culture is created whereby anyone who dares speak against the organization line is slapped down and branded as disloyal, or trouble-making, or belly-aching, or eccentric.

In this miscommunication process free speech is discouraged. Democracy is all right outside work but within the working environment it is forbidden. Dissent is penalized through a process of surreptitious organization pressures. People became afraid to speak up, to challenge the system (the top bosses embodying the system).

The organization might well claim that it has effective communication, for example through briefing groups. But it is an illusion. It effectively has miscommunication. Vital information is not relayed up and down the line while other information becomes distorted if not corrupted in the battle to win the bosses or the employees' hearts and minds.

Senior people delude themselves that they know what's going on, relying on anecdotal evidence to analyse the problem. They effectively guess. They have no reliable information coming up through the line because middle managers 'filter out' and distort 'disagreeable' information they think top bosses won't like.

Senior people also delude themselves that they know what's best for their people, especially in terms of communication. So they sit round board-room tables devoting the odd minute or two to pretending to determine what they should communicate to employees. They merely guess at their employees' information needs.

Down below in the absence of meaningful information (which briefing systems never provide) people rely on the grapevine and gossip to sustain their interest.

The end-result is a huge credibility gap between senior executives and their employees. Mechanistic communications might be in place, but in fact there is miscommunication. An erosion of integrity takes place, distrust and disbelief permeates the organization and performance suffers as a result.

Middle managers merely become ineffective two-way lobbyists, trying ineffectively to communicate to employees by mechanistic means an organization message they don't believe in (because no one's really explained it to them – or sought their commitment) and also trying to communicate up the line issues in which their senior bosses are not interested. As such middle-managers become expensive but ineffectual messengers.

Such miscommunication is the source of much malaise and managerial incompetence in many organizations.

There is a solution. It requires an inordinate amount of time, effort and resource to be devoted to effective employee communications. There is no more complex a process than employee communications.

Incredibly good bosses for a start establish the main purpose of any communication process they embark upon. Having identified the purpose they then decide upon the most appropriate method for that communication (see Table 1 overleaf). There is a whole range of methods available.

For example, if the boss decides to hold a regular Monday morning team briefing he or she has to decide:

1. Is it for passing information down the line?
2. Is it for passing information up the line?
3. Is it for consultation?
4. Is it a participative process for making decisions?
5. Will there be an agenda?
6. Or will the meeting be completely unstructured?
7. Who attends?
8. How long will it last?
9. Is it sit down, stand up? Will there be coffee?
10. Where will the meeting take place?

The incredibly good boss in fact will plan a whole series of regular meetings. These might include:

1. weekly team briefings for exchange of information;
2. monthly team progress review meetings;
3. monthly 'one hour' progress review sessions with each individual in the team;
4. fortnightly unstructured working lunches to 'chew the cud';
5. three-monthly policy determination meetings; six-monthly 'awaydays' to develop long-term visions;
6. annual get-togethers to celebrate achievements.

Those who lead to succeed devote a major part of their time to establishing effective communications.

'The first I knew about it was Monday morning when the union representative came up to me and asked me what I thought about my new boss. "What new boss?" I asked. I didn't even know my old boss had gone, let alone that I had a new one. It's just typical of this company.'

Table 1 Communications

	The main purposes of communication	*Examples of method to achieve purpose*
1	Disseminating information to employees	company newspapers
2		team briefings
3		notices
4		videos
5	*(downwards communications)*	conferences
6		walkabouts

Table 1 cont.

7	Disseminating information to individuals	telephone
8		memos
9		informal face-to-face
10	*(downwards communications)*	formal face-to-face
11		reports
12	Listening	group meetings
13	*(upwards communications)*	walkabouts
14		informal face-to-face
15		group meetings
16		awaydays
17	Consultation	working lunches
18	*(What d'you think?)*	objective setting (MBO)
19		impromptu meetings
20		telephone
21		memos
22	Participation	workshops
23	*(Involvement)*	involvement on projects
24		delegation
25	Negotiation *(2 sides make deal)*	pay negotiations
26	Employee development	training courses
27		induction
28	*(Improvement processes)*	individual counselling
29		performance appraisal
30		seminars

3

Beliefs

'Leadership is a set of beliefs.'

No person can lead effectively without having evolved and continuing to evolve a clear set of beliefs:

- a belief on how to motivate people;
- a belief on how to treat people;
- a belief on how to reward people;
- a belief on how to manage individual performance;
- a belief on how to relate to members of the team;
- a belief on how to communicate with people (for example openly and honestly).

The beliefs extend beyond philosophy to:

- a belief in your team;
- a belief in the product and services your organization provides;
- a belief in your boss;
- a belief in your colleagues.

And to lead successfully the beliefs have to include:

- a belief that you can overcome all manner of problems including those which, at first sight, seem impossible to solve;
- a belief that you can succeed in achieving your vision.

And of course:

- a belief in yourself.

A set of beliefs is the key to success. Credibility can only be conferred on bosses who are clear about their beliefs and can put them into practice.

It is beliefs that form the basis of integrity, for integrity is a totality whereby a person's words are consistent with his or her actions, and these actions are consistent with beliefs held and professed.

Managers who fail tend to be devoid of beliefs or hold the beliefs imprinted upon them by others. Without beliefs one reacts to situations, to pressures from all around. Without beliefs one follows the fashion, samples the flavour of the month, or blows with the wind.

Belief gives strength. The strength to challenge the system, to eradicate organization imperfections, to speak the truth no matter how unpalatable.

Beliefs, however, can be dangerous. They can become fixed in prejudice, in dogma. They can become the sources of self-righteousness, rhetoric and obsession.

One's personal beliefs must be under continual challenge, must evolve, must even change in the light of greater wisdom. Fixed beliefs in management are concomitant with conservatism and reluctance to change. Evolutionary beliefs are essential.

- 100 years ago who believed in employee consultation?
- 100 years ago who believed in management training?
- 80 years ago how many companies believed they should do their best for their employees?
- 40 years ago who believed it was possible to put a man on the moon?
- 20 years ago who believed that executives would have sophisticated desk-top computers?

Beliefs change. Therefore beliefs must be challenged, must evolve in order to provide a sound foundation for decision-making and long-term success.

- Do you really believe that current management practices will prevail in 20 years time?

- Do you really believe that your own personal approach to managing people can be modified and developed over the next two years?

> 'The bosses here don't believe in us any longer. They don't believe what we say because they don't want to. They want to do it their way but they don't know what their way is. We could help them, we've been here a long time and know about this business. But they stick their heads in the sand and not only ignore us but all the problems around. They give us time, yes, but it's only a façade. You can see it in their eyes. Their minds are elsewhere.

One has to differentiate between management fashion and belief. Many current fashions defy belief and require challenging, e.g. fashions relating to performance-related pay which derive from the belief that carrot and stick effectively motivates; and traditional forms of pay negotiation which derive from old-fashioned 'us-and-them' beliefs.

The biggest challenge to you as manager in becoming a successful leader is to explore your current set of beliefs and evolve them into a set of firm convictions which can be put into practice whatever the pressure to do otherwise.

4

Values

'If it's important to you it's part of your value system.'

> 'We've recruited some very bright young people into our store as trainees. We line up for them an excellent training programme and then d'you know what? Our bosses pull them off the course because of staff shortages in the store. They learn nothing. They get demotivated and we lose them within the year.
>
> 'I've been a branch manager for five years now and not been on a single training course. I've never been trained as a manager. Every time I get listed for a course they pull me off. You talk to the training people, they're really disillusioned. They're always cancelling courses because only one or two turn up.
>
> Yet you read this company's recruitment literature and you'd think we have the best training since sliced bread.'

We all have a framework of values. Without it we would become disoriented. To actually live we need to relate to this frame constantly. The frame develops from childhood and derives from perceptions, experiences, personal questioning and learning as well as teachings from parents, relations, school, neighbours, friends and society at large.

Conflicts arise as we become exposed to a wider world and people with different sets of values.

Most frameworks are subconscious and rarely challenged as such. Often without us knowing they are reflected in our behaviours, providing a hidden 'support' system for the steps we take in everyday life. The same applies to management and our working life in organizations.

The skill of the superboss is to drag this framework of values out of the subconscious, challenge it, modify and develop it such that it provides a strong support system for the decisions necessary for organization success. Unless this is done our managerial values will remain hidden from view and risk becoming dissipated, confused and distorted.

Integrity is thus achieved when the framework of values is extracted from the subconscious, exposed, examined, challenged, developed and used for the practical applications of everyday working life as well as for long-term strategic direction.

For example, many regard punctuality as a high value. For others it is not. For them the time of those they keep waiting has less value than their own time.

For many people, customer satisfaction is of high value. For others it is not. For them it is more important to submit a report to the boss by 4.00 p.m. Friday than deal with some difficult customer who rings at 3.45 p.m.

And for those who value punctuality and customer satisfaction there are inherent conflicts. Do you keep the 3.00 p.m. meeting waiting when an important customer rings through at 2.58 p.m.?

The most common conflict in values is between profit and people.

There is no formularized answer. You must constantly reassess your own values and strive to apply them. The worst sin is to be ignorant of your own values and as a consequence bow consistently to those of others.

The best managers have a lifetime's experience evolving their own value system and have achieved success by applying such values consistently on a minute-by-minute basis. These values are often surprising and appear to be at odds with those of the organization. For example, the best bosses often appear to put people before profit.

> 'I'd been in the job six months. During this time my secretary proved incredibly helpful, working long hours and really putting herself out to help me. One Friday I brought her in a bouquet of flowers as a gesture of appreciation. She burst into tears; she was overwhelmed. It was the first time in 20 years in this company that anyone had made such a gesture of appreciation let alone said thank you. That was two weeks ago – she's still telling me the flowers are alive.'

Organization values are frequently not articulated and have to be deduced through informal interpretation. Yet clearly expressed values are essential as the basis for all business decisions.

Without conscious values decision-making becomes random and reactive, undermining the confidence of employees as well as customers.

5

Vision

'It is incredible how many bosses don't know where they are going.'

Many bosses don't even think about where they are going. Why? Because they are forever reacting. Reacting to memos, to telephone calls, to people knocking on their doors, to demands from customers, to pressures from their own bosses, to the latest bureaucratic fad. They are forever filling in forms, signing forms, writing reports, dictating memos, sitting in meetings, attending committees, rushing from one room to another, idling in traffic jams, wasting time seeking parking places, getting frustrated by delayed trains and planes. They rarely create the time and space to think.

It takes time and space to evolve with their team a vision of what has to be achieved over the next few years, to establish a clear sense of direction. All successful leaders have clearly articulated visions of success which they evolve with their people and communicate with passion to everyone else in the organization.

The essence of the vision must be simplicity. It must be articulated in a few key words. It might be a vision of having the most friendly and efficient staff in the region, or of achieving the best sales results in the country, or of reducing customer complaints to an all-time low, or of improving response times by 25 per cent.

The vision is a set of one or two key objectives which you passionately believe must be achieved for the future success of the organization.

The trouble with conventional methods of setting objectives (Management by objectives, or MBO) is that the process becomes too bureaucratic, too meaningless. Objectives are invented for the sake of completing a form. Contrived objectives are soon forgotten about. Such objectives are frequently bland and vague and carry little conviction with either boss or subordinate. If such objectives are geared to performance and pay, then further distortions occur as subordinates contrive to set easily achieved objectives in an attempt to maximize pay. Such bureaucratic manipulations are far removed from the over-riding aims of the organization.

The difference between a conventional objective and a vision of success is a passionate conviction about what has to be achieved. The conviction is so strongly held that it can readily be communicated in simple terms and with a high degree of enthusiasm to the larger part of the organization. It does not necessarily have to be written down. The important thing is to embark on a programme of communication and education whereby every single employee can identify with and share in the accomplishment of the vision. To be successful as an organization, to be successful as a boss, success must mean something to every employee; it must be something every employee can contribute to. This can never happen with long lists of objectives meticulously recorded on MBO worksheets once a year. It can only happen when 'becoming the best' has real meaning for the floor-sweeper, telephonist, receptionist, warehouse supervisor, systems programmer as well as middle manager and chief executive. It can only happen when all these employees have freedom and scope to achieve this vision of being the best and doing the best for the customer.

> 'Despite all the platitudes that come out of the top I don't think this company knows where it's going. They change their minds constantly, it's one flavour after another. If you go six weeks without them introducing some new gimmick you think you've got stability. It's incredible the things they keep on inventing to waste our time!'

Ownership of the vision throughout the organization is crucial. That can never be accomplished by a mechanistic MBO process.

Bosses attain credibility by having a clear sense of direction, a clear vision and then taking action to achieve it. People like to know where their boss is going, for where their boss goes they go too. If they don't know where their boss is going, or don't like the way he or she is going then they will tend to go their own way. This leads to the divisiveness that exists in many organizations. Personnel pushes management training, manufacturing ignores management training. Finance introduces cost controls which sales and marketing circumvent by devious budgetary ploys.

For senior executives one of the most critical tasks is carefully to evolve and communicate a clear vision of success which they are confident their employees will be passionately committed to achieving. There is no place for form-filling in this process.

6

Standards

'Outer standards reflect a person's inner standards.'

Don't let eccentric dress and mannerisms mislead you. The punk with green hair might well have higher ethical standards than you, and you should not assume otherwise. The fact that you dress in a non-standard way should be no reflection of your competence or integrity, albeit if you swore or blasphemed it would be.

In establishing credibility as a manager you must clearly demonstrate your own inner as well as outer standards. Standards of punctuality, courtesy and openness are equally as important as standards of report-writing, financial analysis and stand-up presentation.

Integrity is maintained when these standards are clearly under-stood, accepted by all and seen to be maintained consistently. The boss sets the standard to which the team works. If you are late the others will be late. If you are rude in all probability others will be too. Slovenly behaviour becomes the norm and standards slip. Credibility is reduced.

Standards of openness, honesty and caring for people are less readily visible and consequently have to be pro-actively pursued. Reputations are established by the degree to which a manager adheres to the standards subscribed to informally by the team. Excellence is achieved when the boss manages to raise these standards to the highest possible level and sets the lead in behav-ing accordingly.

'I don't know why I took this job really. I imagined it might be some sort of challenge to change the mess they were in. On arriving on the first day, reception knew nothing about me, wouldn't let me in. Eventually I got a pass when someone from Personnel came down. I then discovered my new boss was away. His secretary didn't know what to do with me so she parked me in a vacant office. It was a new department I had to set up, but I had no team and no papers. My arrival had not been announced. I tried to talk to people but they were all very busy and politely ushered me away. My new boss turned up four days later. He had thought I was going to join in a month's time. It was just incredible!'

Standards should relate to every facet of the business, whether it be answering the telephone or conducting a board meeting. They cannot be prescribed through policy or manual but only set through clear behavioural example. As such, standards come from within.

As a manager you need to examine clearly your own personal standards in the conduct of your work and ensure that these are consistent with your beliefs and values as well as those of the team.

Such consistency in the application of standards is the basis on which competence and credibility is built by incredibly good bosses.

7

Openness

'Openness is a function of certainty .'

To be open in management one needs to be certain of oneself and of other people. Conversely closing up is a function of uncertainty.

To be totally open is impossible. Even among intimates there will always be thoughts best kept to oneself. One can never be certain that a revelation of certain thoughts will not alienate.

One avoids alienation by closing up. And that in turn alienates. People like to know what you really think – providing it doesn't really hurt them – in which case they will reject what you think, thus defeating the purpose of being open – to help. They will think badly of you for thinking badly of them.

To be open therefore appears to be a vicious trap, similarly to be closed.

On balance openness is essential for successful management. But it can be incredibly dangerous. People need to be certain of your thoughts as a boss. But you have to be certain of your own thoughts before you speak and act. In the every-day rush few bosses have the time to develop the certainty of their own thoughts. The result is they don't think – at best adopting other people's thoughts. People then guess at the reasons behind the boss's action. Reasons are not given because it is alleged there is no time to, or that they are confidential. But the real reason is elsewhere. The reason is that it is *not* the reason of the immediate boss. In the rush he or she is unable to substantiate the reasons forced upon him or her from on high. So the boss closes up, unable to be open about such an unreasonable stance. Credibility and integrity are rapidly eroded.

In an open organization the boss is open to the possibility that other people have better reasons than he or she, and that other people have different views too.

Integrity demands openness. It demands a cohesion between thoughts, words and actions. It demands that one's thoughts, words and actions can be modified under reason from others. Suppress the words by closing up and you will create uncertainty and you will alienate. People will guess at the thoughts behind the action. Frequently they guess wrong. Then the boss will have a second-order communication problem to cope with.

Refusal to consider other people's thoughts and words will also create a second-order reaction.

The successful boss creates certainty by encouraging the exposure of his own and other people's thoughts and feelings, suppressing only those of an intimate nature. When the boss has thoughts which might well offend or cause a person to lose face then he will think again. There is a delicate trade between openness and the preservation of a person's inner dignity. While there is always a risk that your innermost thoughts might well offend your aim should never be to do so. You should attempt before speaking, to represent your thoughts in a way that the recipient will find helpful. Often it is not the 'fact' that offends but the 'way' you present the fact.

Openness therefore not only relates to the substance of the expression but also to the manner of it. Credible bosses succeed in their openness by developing a positive and constructive manner for the open communication of what could otherwise be unpalatable truths. Poor bosses demotivate their staff by being open in a crude and destructive way – in these cases openness becomes a put-down. In these cases staff often reject the substance of what is essentially true and are left to concoct, through guesswork, more palatable but hypothetical answers.

Without time to think, one opens oneself to the possibility of an emotionally negative reaction to the imperfection and misses an opportunity for constructive improvement.

Being open takes time: time to work through your own interpretation of the facts in relation to performance, and time to establish the most positive way of communicating these facts openly and honestly. Without thinking this through you cannot be certain of your own interpretation of the facts nor of the reaction to the communication by the recipient.

Openness takes a lot of practice. Effectively you have to test the market. The more you reveal your innermost thoughts and feelings – albeit in a positive, constructive as well as succinct way – the more confidence will be gained by others. A balance has to be struck on what it is important to be open about and what is not. Those who go on and on about themselves abuse the listener with trivia. You should only open up when your listener is genuinely interested in what you have to say.

'We never saw our boss, never knew what was going on. So we all signed a letter saying we wanted a meeting with him. We were fearful of his reaction. He agreed the meeting and we tried to be friendly and polite. We told him our concerns, that we'd like to see more of him, know what was going on.

'He was surprised. He had never realized. He has consciously changed now. We see a lot of him – sometimes too much. But morale is much higher. There is much more mutual support and respect.'

Openness is an essential requisite for the superboss and is essentially a function of the person rather than the organization.

When you open up your thoughts to a receptive listener you not only improve the relationship but potentially improve performance.

8

Truth and honesty

'The truth exists. It is a fact. Honesty is that painful process of revealing it.'

> 'He wasn't straight with me. He called me in and flattered me. He said he really needed me for this vitally important systems co-ordination job. I've been in it for two months now. It's a non-job. I don't really know what's expected of me. I never see him. No one's really interested. It's unbelievable.'

If the truth be known many managers would lose their credibility overnight. They are not honest with their people, let alone with themselves. They don't know how to be honest, they don't know what honesty is. They fail to differentiate between fact and opinion, between cause and effect. They evolve perceptions of the truth coloured by value judgements which are often in conflict with others' perception of the same truth.

Bosses often attempt to protect their people from the painful truth. In doing so they are frequently judged dishonest. Bosses often hide their thoughts about their people from their people. In doing so they are again frequently judged dishonest. Bosses often fear that people will not accept the real reason behind their decisions. So they invent more plausible reasons in an attempt to get acceptance. But in doing so they are often judged dishonest.

Honesty is a quest for the absolute truth. Misused it can be a destructive force. It can shatter people's inner dignity, it can destroy their confidence.

If your assistant waffles on, lets meetings drift to an interminable end, bores you with the same old anecdotes, the probability is you will not and cannot be honest with him or her.

If your secretary gossips too much, lets you down from time to time, is absent a little too much, the probability is you will not and cannot be completely honest with him or her about your real thoughts.

'For two years we pestered him about getting this new sales project off the ground. He was always against it. In the end he reluctantly conceded and allowed us to get on with it. We really worked hard on the project and to be honest it was amazingly successful. We increased our market share by 5 per cent. What really annoys me is that now, whenever he gets up on the platform, he declares it as one of his major achievements. He makes out it was his idea and that he personally accomplished it. I just grit my teeth and clench my fist every time I hear him say this.'

Honesty is a struggle. Bravado in 'speaking your mind' achieves little if you alienate everyone around you. The process of being honest is as equally important as being honest.

The worst bosses avoid being honest because the process is too painful. They fear the reaction of their people to the truth. Furthermore they fear it may not be the truth, that they will be exposed for having inadvertently distorted it. Worse still they fear the truth about themselves.

Effective leaders seek the solution in the process. By being prepared to admit they are wrong, by being prepared to have their perception of the truth challenged, by welcoming frequent questioning by others as well as themselves, by balancing their views with opposing views, by a constant process of exploration and discovery they seek to approach the truth.

It is not the truth that matters so much as what you do with it once discovered. If you use the truth to destroy people then you achieve nothing. If you use the truth to help people then you achieve a lot. Being honest is that painful process of differentiating between the two. It is an essential process for leaders of integrity.

The pursuit of honesty in management is one of the most painful processes imaginable. It requires a careful process of self-evaluation and self-revelation.

Suspicions mount when you hide yourself. Integrity and credibility is best achieved when you reveal your defective self to all. Such revelations encourage others to reveal their own imperfections and embark on a co-operative effort to address them.

It means revealing your feelings, your hopes, your disappointments and your total thoughts about the work situation and beyond. Once people know these and understand them they will be able to cope with you, and you with them. You will then have a relationship based on integrity. Furthermore you will have credibility.

Inevitably there is a limit to what can be revealed about one's feelings and thoughts on issues beyond the work situation. You will need to draw a careful line between how 'close' you get to your people in encouraging an exchange of feelings and how remote one should be. Either extreme is dangerous.

The way you embark on this process of self-revelation is critical. Be sensitive to the receptiveness of the other person. Don't push too much too fast. Don't embarrass. Let people get to know you at their own pace. And at the same pace make sure you get to know them.

Ideally as a boss you should reveal yourself as a human being. The inherent conflict in this is that the subjective affinities and affections of human beings are sometimes inconsistent with the objective responsibilities of being a boss. It is a difficult balance which only the best bosses manage to achieve.

The preferred approach in being honest with yourself and your people is to concentrate on a mutual exploration of values, beliefs, attitudes, strengths and weaknesses relating to the work situation. As people are encouraged to open up and be honest through your lead in self-revelation you should avoid placing value judgements, either directly or indirectly (through facial signals for example) on other people's revelations. Such value judgements, if bad, will inevitably lead to a loss of face, a loss of confidence and a loss of integrity in the relationship. People feel very vulnerable in revealing their real thoughts and feelings to bosses. This vulnerability should never be exploited. You have to learn to respect other people's feelings. The credible boss develops a degree of sensitivity and understanding about these feelings, no matter how bad they are, and these can often be converted into more positive attitudes in the opening–up process.

In pursuing integrity through self-revelation your objective is twofold. Firstly you can provide constructive help to the other person. And more importantly the other person can help you. It is a process of mutuality.

'My two assistants had really worked hard over the previous four weeks, including giving up two weekends to complete an urgent project. So come Friday I took them out to lunch, nothing too flash, a pizza house, but we enjoyed ourselves. I put in an expense claim for the lunch. It wasn't much, just a few pounds. My boss queried the expense. "If you start claiming for lunches," he admonished me, "then everyone will start doing it." So what I do now is what everyone does. I don't claim the odd special lunch but put in a couple of extra taxi fares when I'm on a trip. He never questions that. It's a game, it's even dishonest in one sense, but what else can I do?'

In revealing your inner self honestly to others you will learn about yourself. In learning about yourself you will be able to eliminate negative feelings, bad attitudes, confused beliefs and take further steps in the essential pursuit of integrity. All will profit.

Integrity exists within you; it means being honest with yourself and this has to be revealed.

9

Trust

'Always start by trusting a person you don't know.'

> 'I tell you how untrusting the bosses are in this place. It takes me a week to get a new pen to write with. When my pen runs out I have to go downstairs, obtain a stationery requisition and complete it – borrowing someone else's pen. I then have to take the requisition upstairs to my boss and get him to sign it. I then have to go downstairs again to the lady who holds the key to the stationery cupboard. I have to leave the requisition in her in-tray as she only deals with stationery requisitions on Tuesday mornings. Meanwhile I beg, borrow or steal someone else's pen. I could use the pens I have at home, but why should I? It's all very petty. I make maintenance decisions costing the company thousands, but they don't trust me with a pen!'

It is as you acquire knowledge of the other person's behaviours that trust is in danger of being eroded; and, conversely, as the other person gains knowledge of you.

Before you can trust anybody you must look at yourself and ask, 'Do people trust me?' The less you trust others the less they will trust you. Trust is often a function of perception and tolerance: perceptions of possible indiscretions; tolerance of imperfections. All these can be perceived as betrayals of trust or conversely as potential for greater understanding and achievement. When superbosses are let down by others they do not think in terms of distrust but more of opportunity. Betrayal is best perceived as a challenge.

As more and more organizations progress towards a devolved style of management trust acquires even greater significance.

Corporate bureaucracies in which large volumes of decisions gravitate towards the centre bestow little trust on local managers who are often constrained from making the simplest expenditure decisions. Conversely those organizations which devolve decision-making towards the front-line bravely carry an increasing risk that people with less skills and experience than their seniors at the centre will make bad decisions. How these bad decisions are handled is crucial in sustaining trust and morale throughout. Encouraging people to make decisions and then castigating mistakes creates a punitive culture of intimidation and fear. Poor decisions should always be perceived as essential learning opportunities which enable long-term business success.

Trust is therefore concomitant with risk-taking and progress. It is concomitant with the leap into the unknown. Progress never comes from a leap into the known. Consequently a forgiving boss is more likely to succeed than an unforgiving one.

To achieve mutual trust, an essential prerequisite of successful leadership, one must encourage genuine mutual forgiveness. Failings should not lead to grudges. Misunderstandings should not lead to resentments. Without forgiveness relationships become poisoned.

Inadvertent failings, through ignorance and innocence, are readily forgiven. A competent boss will strive to protect the organization from further such failings, constraining the innocent from inflicting further damage.

Damage from a betrayal of trust through malevolent intent is less easy to forgive. But who judges whether the intent was malevolent? Most sinners deny the sin. Trust cannot exist where malevolent intent exists. Such intent might be a hidden agenda, ulterior motives, undisclosed reasons, internal politics.

Self-searching honesty is essential to maintain trust. Did you seek to hurt? Did you seek to avoid? Did you seek to inflict damage, cause embarrassment, show someone up, expose a weakness? Did you really go behind that person's back? Did you intend to let that person down? Did you intend to play a game, to indulge in internal politics, to cast aside or put down? Did you deliberately intend to steal another's thunder, or claim their glory, or dismiss their success as if it were your own? If you did any of these, and there are many more, then you cannot be trusted. You erode your integrity.

For the superboss a daily challenge is 'Am I to be trusted today?'

This memo, this telephone call, this meeting, this walkabout, this report, this decision, this speech, this advice. This inaction. Does all this maintain the trust others have in me? Or does it serve to betray their trust?

'Can I do better to maintain their trust?'

Only when you examine your own behaviours and thoughts in relation to the trust others place in you are you entitled to judge the trustworthiness of others.

And then, if you detect any fragment of potentially untrustworthy behaviour, you will be able to confront it. A negative eye movement, a bored sigh, a failure to reply, an abrasive comment, frequent lateness, avoidance, impatience, non-delivery, malingering, aggression, lies, distortions and misconduct, are all types of behaviour which can be construed as evidence of mistrust. The issue should always be confronted rather than avoided for fear of embarrassment. Self-searching honesty by the potential offender must be demanded. An innocent failing, an admission of neglect, an inadvertent slip-up, a misplaced demonstration of aggression, a lapse into cynicism will be readily forgiven if openly admitted.

But if a team-member's malevolent intent is covered up, is denied and then subsequently discovered, then the successful leader inevitably will lose trust. A judgement then has to be made whether that trust can be resuscitated.

The sad fact of life is that there are certain people who can never be trusted. Those people, at the final count, must be ejected from the team.

'Last year I saved the company £3 million on an energy conservation programme. Nobody ever patted me on the back. I didn't even get a thank you from my boss. I never see him anyway. Now I get a word-processed memo from the Chief Executive saying they are introducing devolved management as part of their new style of management. Great! It's what I've been doing for the last few years. The next thing I know I get an instruction from the Finance Director saying that any expenditure over £100 will require a director's approval and that any sub-contracted work worth over £250 will require at least three quotations. He's just taken ten steps backwards. It's ridiculous!'

Happily the majority of people want to be trusted, can be trusted and need to place their trust in their leaders. In such a climate of trust, performance can be incredibly high.

Your challenge as superboss is not to betray that trust. It means trusting yourself as well as challenging that trust every day.

10

Mutual respect

'When you lose respect you lose performance.'

> 'When the roof blew off during the hurricane, our boss was the first in. He helped clear up and worked day and night with us to help erect a temporary roof. When it was all over he took us out for a beer. You don't get many bosses who do that sort of thing.'

Bosses cannot motivate people when there is no mutual respect.

We all have attributes and exhibit behaviours which in a fair and objective world should command respect. Conversely we all have imperfections and limitations which, in the eyes of some, create a degree of disrespect.

Respect is the value we place on another person. We respect positive qualities such as efficiency, hard work, coolness under pressure, courtesy and a pleasant personality. We have no respect for malingering, idleness, panic and constant argumentativeness.

But do we respect those who speak their mind, those who challenge, those who disagree with us? We might respect those who speak their mind but not those who do so in an arrogant, assertive and self-righteous way. We might respect those who challenge us in a quietly helpful way but not those who challenge in a destructive manner. We might respect those who can rationally substantiate their disagreement but not those who support their argument with emotional rhetoric.

Management is full of these quandaries. Respect is built up from an accumulation of perceived behaviours and attributes. Subjectivity enters as we tend to value those who exhibit the same values as us, dismissing those with disparate values.

Integrity in management is better achieved by a greater toleration (and thus respect) of variant values within the organization. The paradox is that such toleration of disparate values frequently leads to an increasing level of shared values. When variant values are openly and honestly discussed and explored the probability is that those values will converge. The imposition of a narrow set of values dictated by a leader cannot lead to superb performance. Integrity is evolutionary. Respect is gained only when you are prepared to listen and can learn to modify your own set of values and beliefs (and therefore behaviours and decisions) in the light of wise arguments from others.

Respect is best derived from humility. Humility assumes that whoever you talk to might know better than you, whether that person be boss, subordinate or colleague.

Mutual respect is achieved when both parties make this assumption. Without it there is an intrusion of prejudice, rhetoric and bigotry as people attempt to impose their perceived greater wisdom on others. It merely serves to alienate and erode respect.

When mutual respect exists both parties are eager to learn from each other, eager to appreciate and value each other's potentially valuable contribution. When mutual respect exists both parties will recognize an integrity in the relationship in which words are consistent with actions, and actions with beliefs. When mutual respect exists there is no incongruity between behaviour, statement and thought.

When mutual respect exists the smile of the boss has a transparent meaning, it is not a device concealing other thoughts. When mutual respect exists the boss welcomes and carefully considers the criticism from below – accepting it as meaningful and constructive rather than negative and points–scoring.

When mutual respect exists the managing director treats front-line people as equals. The market might place different financial values on their jobs, but the managing director genuinely values their contribution and respects them all as unique human beings with much to offer.

> 'I made a mistake early on, really let my boss down. I regretted it. But he took the stick for me. I knew he got the rap from senior management – he looked that grim. But he didn't take it out on me. He took me aside and said, "I think we've both got some lessons to learn." I respected him for that. He could so easily have fired me. We've never looked back since.'

As soon as a boss becomes dismissive, dismissing the contribution of others, a rot will set in. Mutual disrespect will become endemic. Integrity will erode and performance will suffer.

The superboss leads the way by seeking to respect the people who work in the team. In that way mutual respect is developed. It can be a painstaking process, but it is the only way.

11

Caring

'Managerial competence and credibility can never be achieved without care.'

Eighty per cent of the people in eighty per cent of the organizations I visit claim they have bosses who don't care. They claim their bosses don't communicate with them, don't involve them, don't trust them, don't give them time, don't take a personal interest in them.

Low retention rates, low morale, malingering and strikes are frequent manifestations of bosses who don't care.

Unions are supposed to care, more so than the bosses, they claim. Personnel officers are supposed to care, more so than most, they claim.

Credibility can only be attained when the immediate line boss cares as much for the team and the individuals in it as others do – whether those others be union representatives or from the personnel department.

Credibility is diminished if you, as a boss, attempt to care for the customer without first caring for your people. It is your people who best achieve excellent standards of customer care. But how can they care for the customer if you don't care for them? A huge credibility gap arises when you care more for the customer than for your staff.

A vital part of the superboss's philosophy, in the pursuit of integrity, is the priority placed on caring. It is a totally caring approach to all people, customers, suppliers and employees alike, in which he or she genuinely cares to give people time, to help them through their problems. No matter how trivial the problems appear to the boss, if those problems seem important to his or her people the boss will help out.

> 'He was one of the best bosses I've ever had. His door was always open. He had an amazing way of keeping in touch. You could take personal issues to him and he would help out. If your wife was ill he'd send flowers. He really cared. His successor is appalling. She fails to give us any support, she never takes an interest. I just can't stand her. I would never take a problem to her.'

The superboss cares to listen, to understand, to take action, to give advice, to show an interest. He or she cares to say thank you, to demonstrate her confidence in people by trusting them. Superbosses care because they value their people.

Credibility can never be achieved unless you genuinely care for your people. The most successful bosses care the most while the others just don't care.

12

Practising what you preach

'Many bosses don't preach let alone practise what they preach.'

All organizations have missions. Exploring new markets, developing new products, increasing productivity and profitability, becoming a caring organization, achieving managerial excellence can all be missions.

All organizations have cultures based on an evolved set of principles (including values) which are generally assimilated and understood by most employees.

The mission has to be communicated so that all employees understand where the company's going and can contribute accordingly. The principles should also be formally communicated to avoid possible misunderstandings.

Communicating the mission and underlying principles is the preaching bit.

More frequently missions and principles are not clearly articulated because while they actually do exist, no one, even at the top, has clearly established what they are. When this happens practice varies widely as people make their own local interpretations of where the company is going and what its underlying values are.

When an organization does publish its mission and principles, credibility and integrity are often eroded because the bosses at the

51

top do not practise what they preach. Their behaviours and decisions appear inconsistent with their published statements. It is no good declaring that you aim to be the best in the market-place if you don't educate your people on what you mean by the best.

It is no good stating that you value high performance when your personnel systems are so archaic that it is the low performers who stay on and are protected while the high performers leave.

It is no good saying people are the organization's greatest asset if you do little to invest in them through excellent pay levels, superb environment and the very best training. The probability is that the executives who publish these motherhood statements do the opposite, screwing down their people on pay, conditions, training, communications and other things. This is despite 'the value they place on their employees'.

> 'There was a proposal that the airline should put flowers into its first-class cabin. The planning people came up with the cost and the board turned the proposal down. One of our senior stewardesses, a lovely lady who's been with the airline many years grows roses at her little cottage in the country. She'd been on this training course about taking initiatives to please the customers. So on every flight she was on she brought in a vase and a few roses to adorn the first-class cabin. One day her boss, the Cabin Services Manager travelled on her flight. At the end of the flight she was disciplined for breaking regulations as it was against company policy to have flowers in the first-class cabin. So much for initiative and innovation in this airline. She was amazed. She is one of the best stewardesses we have, the passengers just love her.'

Credibility can only be achieved when you practise what you preach every single minute of the day. To achieve this you must constantly challenge yourself on what you believe, on what you preach and on what you do.

When what you do is in accordance with what you preach and that is in accordance with what you

believe, then you're practising what you preach. Your credibility and competence will undoubtedly be high and you will be one of that minority of superbosses who lead to succeed.

13

Consultation: the reality vs. the myth

'You cannot consult all the people all the time. That way no decisions get made.'

> 'We have people at the top now who go around imposing policies which won't work. They don't consult and they don't have the experience we have at the sharp end of what the customer wants. We all have over ten years' experience meeting customer requirements. Now it's all being thrown out of the window by this new regime. They think they know better, but they don't.'

To achieve credibility and respect a good boss has to learn when to consult and when to make decisions. Some of the worst bosses spend all their time consulting, deferring difficult issues to steering groups, working parties and committees. They seem to think that the best way to make the decision is to wait until everyone agrees on what it should be. It's an illusory and mythical process. It's very rare that you can get everyone to agree. As a result decisions get delayed or not made while different factions argue it out. Sometimes, when time expires, the steering group, or working party is forced to make a decision or recommendation. What then happens is that the views of the more powerful members of the group hold sway while the others defer, albeit only giving lip-service support to their decision.

This all happens with indecisive bosses. They go in for excessive consultation. They avoid making difficult decisions by spending much of their time deferring upwards, downwards or sideways.

They even consult people who know little if anything about the subject.

The best bosses are also consultative. But they only consult the following groups of people:

1. people they trust and whose advice they value;
2. people who have specific expertise on the issue;
3. people whose work and lives will be affected directly as a consequence of the decision.

Having carefully listened to these people and taking their views into account, the best bosses will make a clear-cut decision.

The best bosses do *not* consult the following:

1. people they do not trust (upwards, sideways, downwards or externally);
2. people who have no specific expertise on the issue;
3. people who are merely interested in the decision (for interest's sake) but whose work and lives will not be affected directly as a consequence of the decision.

The key to effective decision-making through consultation is to ensure that you have people around you whom you genuinely trust. The best bosses are those who develop a high degree of trust and therefore credibility through the organization. Trust is best achieved with open and honest communication. But it requires more than that. It means the boss has to clearly work through his or her own values and beliefs and ensure that these are understood and ideally shared by those around him or her.

Many bosses fail despite their attempts to consult, because they do not make evident their beliefs and values. This leads to mistrust and doubts. If these values and beliefs are unclear the person proffering advice will in turn be unclear how the advice will be received. The danger then is that he or she 'guesses' at the advice the boss wants and how it will be received. The boss similarly is not sure how to receive the advice, not trusting the person giving it, not sure of that person's beliefs and values. The boss will therefore tend to receive conflicting advice.

'She likes to think she's a consultative boss, that she delegates. So on any major issue she sets up a "consultative" working group, saying "I'm delegating responsibility to you for coming up with recommendations." Three months later when the working group reports back she starts nit-picking the report, finding fault in this, wanting to change that. She rarely accepts our recommendations. She's always twisting and turning them to suit her own aims. It's all a bit of a farce really. In fact I find it incredible!'

Relationships are best established, and people get on best when they share beliefs and values. This produces a good climate for consultation and effective decision-making. Without such a climate consultation becomes mechanistic and meaningless. Decision-making becomes ineffective.

It therefore is essential, if you want to become an incredibly good boss, to think through your own beliefs and values and share those with your people as well as attempt to understand their beliefs and values, working towards a commonality over a period of time. You can hardly expect to receive sound advice, through consultation, if you haven't previously elicited the beliefs and values of those from whom you are seeking advice.

Distrust is endemic in modern management. As a result consultation, if it takes place, is often mechanistic and ineffective. This leads to poor decisions and potential organization failure.

14

The dangers of cosmetic training

'Training is a good thing, therefore people shall have training.'

It doesn't matter what training people are given as long as it's training. The shopping list comes round and you choose, outward bound or presentation skills, whatever takes your fancy. It all sounds very good.

A few days' training is an excellent escape from the drudgery of being stuck in the office. What's more you even feel pretty good at the end of it.

A day later when you return to work you realize nothing much will change. After all, it's your senior bosses who really need the training you've just received, but they're too busy to attend and in any case they think they know it all already. If they'd had their way in the first place you wouldn't have gone on the course, preferring you to be back at the desk pumping out paper. But they let you go because something tells them training is good and their consciences feel bad unless they make a token gesture in this direction. Furthermore they want to appease you.

Mind you, having agreed to the course they don't bother to take an interest either before or after, not finding time to ask you what you got out of it nor how it can be applied.

Such is the prevailing attitude to be found in many organizations that get as far as spending money on training. Training in fact becomes a cosmetic exercise. There are worse organizations who spend a pittance if not nothing on training.

The veneer of training that takes place in many organizations serves only to reduce the credibility of senior executives who proudly proclaim that people are the company's most important asset.

The so-called training professionals don't help, often pushing courses that are academic and bear little practical relationship to the realities of the business. Far worse, many training instructors are drop-outs from the line, people who lack the necessary inspiration and charisma to do a superb job in front of a class.

Training is expensive, not only in terms of money but time. The incredibly successful companies invest a substantial amount of resource in training which is carefully designed to meet both individual and corporate needs.

Superbosses also invest a substantial amount of time in training themselves and then spending time with their people to ensure they receive meaningful training. They follow through to help ensure that the lessons learnt can be applied to the good of the organization as well as the individual. Credible bosses even sit in on training courses and contribute where appropriate.

Training acquires immense value in successful companies. And it's so important it applies to every single employee. In an ever-changing dynamic world everyone needs to be educated and informed about the changes taking place in the company and how these apply to their jobs.

Management training can never be a 'once-off' whereby you attend a programme of courses and learn it all. Management training should be an on-going process in which one's approach is constantly challenged, developed and refined.

Training therefore should be at the core of the management philosophy of any successful organization. In applying this philosophy there are a number of 'needs' areas which have to be carefully identified before selecting the appropriate training:

1. Corporate needs

   When major changes take place in an organization it is essential to develop an awareness in all employees of how these changes relate to their jobs. For example a major drive on improving customer satisfaction.

2. Department needs

   Where changes are specific to the department, for example the introduction of a new computer system or accounts procedure.

3. Individual attitudinal needs

   Where a person needs to develop specific attitudes to enhance performance on the job, for example assertive, innovative, risk-taking, positive and entrepreneurial attitudes.

4. Individual skill needs

   Where an individual's performance on the job can be improved by the development of certain skills, for example report-writing, chairing meetings, financial analysis.

5. Individual experience needs

   Where a person needs additional experience to improve his or her job performance, for example experience of negotiations or selling.

6. Individual career development

   Where a person needs to be prepared for a prospective job in the future, for example preparing a senior operator for a supervisory position, or a supervisor for management.

7. Philosophical needs

   Where an individual needs to become aware of some underlying principles relating to the company and to his or her work, for example the company's core values relating to employee relations and management.

There is much to be said for the approach adopted by many public service organizations that an individual should not be promoted to a specific leadership position without having first undertaken the requisite training and passed the relevant examination. For example in the Fire and Rescue Service no one becomes a chief fire officer without having *first* successfully attended a lengthy command course. To get to the top there is a whole regime of training to be undertaken.

> 'They recruited me as a graduate trainee. After the induction training programme I was told I would be spending three-month periods in various departments. My first port of call I was told would be finance. I turned up that Monday morning to find that nobody in finance knew anything about me. It took them three days to get something sorted out. Finance blamed personnel, personnel blamed finance. Eventually they put me in with a lady who produced the monthly sales statements. She was so busy she never had time to explain anything to me. I just trailed her around and felt useless if not guilty for getting in her way.'

Regrettably in large numbers of commercial organizations many executives get to the top without having undertaken a day's management training in their life. It shows. With few exceptions they are the incompetent bosses who have never been taught and never learnt how important people are in the business. They are the unbelievably bad bosses who think profit only and everything else should be secondary to that.

The credible boss first and foremost puts his or her people first. This means taking a genuine interest in all members of the team. It means doing his or her best for them and devoting a lot of time to this. It means making sure that they are trained to the highest standards in preparation for future success.

15

Courage of convictions

'When you are in a minority of one it takes immense courage to stand on a principle rejected by the thousands around you.'

'We've been under-resourced for two years now. They keep on screwing us down saying we have to be even more cost-conscious. On Saturday morning we only have two women on the counter. We should have five. We lose customers who can't be bothered to wait. What's worse we have a security problem. The women take in thousands in cash. They really are vulnerable, especially when one only is left on the counter while the other goes to the toilet. For two years I've complained, requesting additional resources, asking for more security protection. I've just met a brick wall from my bosses. They don't even reply to my memos. I have a big fat file of them.

'Last Saturday one woman went sick, so we only had one on the counter. She was attacked and robbed. We've shut up shop now on Saturdays. Meanwhile I'm under suspension for incompetence while they investigate. I'm just a scapegoat.'

Many managers give in. They do things which they are not quite sure are right because there is immense pressure to do so.

As a result trade unions are misinformed with half-truths, customers are given excuses and employees are misled with exhortative propaganda. Managers mislead because they are under pressure from their senior bosses to mislead. No one ever admits it because reasons are simulated for putting cash before safety (underground station disaster), productivity before safety (ferry disaster) and low wage costs before employee care (the latest strike).

Eighty per cent of the managers I meet are unhappy. They feel they have to compromise their principles to do things they don't believe in because if they don't they fear their senior bosses will put a black mark against them and restrict their salary and promotion prospects, if not find some excuse for firing them. So managers toe the line and conform to the semi-corrupt values of the system and with diminishing regret (as they make excuses for themselves) they subconsciously compromise their principles. They produce products that can kill (tobacco), tell lies to their employees ('we cannot afford to increase the pay offer' – only to increase it under threat of strike four weeks later), and they relegate safety and welfare to such a low priority that it is rarely discussed at board level.

While they all know better they indulge their obsessions for short-term cost-cutting and draconian profit-improvement measures. The 'hatchet man' becomes the hero, the caring leader is portrayed as soft.

The logic is clear. They need the job, they need the money, so they compromise their principles. They have families back home to provide for and huge mortgage repayments to make. Why jeopardize all that by standing on principle? Far better surely to succumb to the institutionalized semi-corrupt practices of the organization. Short-cuts and expediency become the order of the day as fast bucks are sought at the expense of the customer and employee.

So integrity is shattered and credibility reduced. To stand on principle becomes an unacceptable process, even the thought of it is excruciatingly painful. So people don't think as they harm others. Far easier to produce the cigarettes than think about the suffering caused as a result.

The frightening thing is that managers get sucked into institutionalized behaviours by which they automatically and unthinkingly compromise key principles they have evolved since childhood. They might teach their own sons and daughters to tell the truth but at the office they slide into dishonesty, telling people there is no money in the pot when there is, telling suppliers the cheque is in the post when it isn't. They might teach their kids to display respect towards others but within the organization they readily show disrespect, turning up late for meetings, rubbishing their bosses behind their backs. They might teach their children to avoid unsafe practices but as executives they assign low priority to safety, rarely discussing it at board level. Rivers do get polluted, cars do not get serviced properly, mistakes do get covered up, short-cuts are taken.

'Our previous boss was a little outspoken but always very honest with us. We respected him. I think his problem was he spoke his mind to the directors, he told them things they didn't want to hear. That's why we think he lost his job.

'Our new boss is a wheeler-dealer; we don't trust him one inch. He just doesn't command the respect of our previous boss. I think the work suffers in the end.'

At the final count, having the courage of your convictions means putting your job on the line. It means taking a stand against bad practices in the organization. It means refusing to succumb to organization pressures to mislead your staff. It means resisting calls to 'fob off' customers with excuses for late delivery or poor quality. It means standing by your people when others want to use them as scapegoats.

It means confronting bosses who attempt to intimidate you and your team with fierce looks and threats. It means speaking up when others tend towards silence. It means doing what you believe is right when the rules and regulations appear wrong. It means resisting the temptation to be popular when all evidence points to the right decision being unpopular. It means being true to yourself as opposed to being blindly faithful to senior bosses with semi-corrupt values.

It means being prepared to sacrifice a handsome salary, prospects for promotion and, what's more, risk putting your family on the hardship line.

To have the courage of your convictions is to tell the union the truth at all times. To have the courage of your convictions is to tell your boss that you believe he or she is wrong.

To have the courage of your convictions is to say 'I resign' when you have failed to change the bad practices within the organization and they become intolerable to your way of working and your conscience.

'Other managers just sit back and let their budgets be imposed upon them. They put up a pretext of a fight and then passively accept the cut-back on resources, moaning behind their directors' backs that they don't have enough resource to do the job.

'I never complain about resource because I always fight for the resource I genuinely need. And I invariably get it. It's how you make the case, and you don't play games either. They know me better than to screw me down for the sake of some global budget strategy. I might have a reputation with the directors as being difficult but I get the results they want – and that's because they would never cross me on an issue of resource.'

In reality few resign for it is those who have the courage of their convictions who tend to succeed, who have the ability to persuade others of the correct course of action. Popularity is not synonymous with respect. Bosses who have the courage of their convictions are those who, in the long term, tend to gain respect, albeit in the short term they might lose popularity.

To stand on principle, to have the courage of your convictions is one of the key challenges to be faced in becoming successful as a manager.

16

Recognizing one's own deficiencies

*'The biggest deficiency you can have is the failure
to recognize your own deficiencies.'*

The need to become aware of one's own defects is stressed time
and time again throughout this book. Lack of such awareness is
the most common cause of organizational failure and disaster.

'I had sensed there was something wrong with the team for a long
time, but could never get to the root cause of it. I prided myself on
being a hard-working, communicative boss whose door was always
open and who was always honest with his staff. If someone in the
team wanted a decision I would never fob them off, they would get the
decision virtually then and there.

'Even so I sensed my people were unhappy. When I asked them what
was wrong I just drew blank faces and they changed the subject,
pretending nothing was wrong.

'So I hired in this consultant to facilitate a team-building awayday.
What he elicited from the team, in my presence, shocked me. I think
they hated me! They said I was always putting excessive pressures on
them, that I was always making them feel guilty – working much
longer hours than they, that I never really listened – only going
through the pretence of consultation and always preferring my own
ideas to theirs.

'I had thought I was a great boss, was doing all the right things by my
team. I had had this highly sanitized image of myself as being the
perfect boss. When I discovered the reverse it was traumatic. But I
think I'm a better person for it now.'

There is not a manager alive who does not have imperfections and deficiencies. But there are millions who think otherwise. Admitting important deficiencies enhances credibility and competence while reluctance to do so diminishes credibility and competence.

A fundamental in the philosophical core of all successful bosses is the quest to identify and eliminate their own imperfections and deficiencies. Like spots on faces such defects are often temporary. You can be in a state of perfect managerial health today and reveal gross defects tomorrow. Such elimination therefore is an on-going process. We are all capable of becoming increasingly imperfect tomorrow.

Disaster, defeat and all forms of corporate collapse have deep roots in the hidden imperfections and deficiencies of those corporate leaders. They fail to listen, they fail to take advice, they fail to understand their people, they fail to understand the competition. They get lost in chauffeur-driven cars, get blinded by a dazzle of hospitality, get hooked by the bait of their own illusory power. They lose touch, get out of control, simulate control through status and sycophants and finally, devoid of any integrity and credibility, lead their people out of business. There are many examples. We are all capable of such self-inflicted blindness, deafness and numbing insensitivity.

My words are not exaggerated. You do not have to look far to discover the inadequacies of most managers. You do not have to look far to discover the hidden causes of corporate collapse.

When things go wrong don't look at others, just look at yourself.

Part 3

PSYCHOLOGY

None of us is perfect. Our behaviours reflect a complex psychological process to help overcome our many imperfections as managers.

●

Paradoxically however, in attempting to overcome our imperfections we frequently damage our integrity and credibility in the eyes of others.

●

This part of the book examines many facets of this psychological process.

●

Furthermore it suggests various ways of harnessing these complex psychological processes to develop one's integrity, credibility and therefore one's prospects of becoming an incredibly successful boss.

1

Emotional management

'The most untapped source of organization energy is emotion.'

Intelligence is always in limited supply. However you define it some of us have less of it than others. Sometimes our supply of intelligence is inadequate to meet a personal objective. Our reaction then, rightly or wrongly is to supplement our limited intellectual resources with a boost of emotional energy. Most of us have vast reserves of emotional energy. Many of us, especially from 'non-Latin' backgrounds are brought up to suppress such energies.

Over the last few decades the convention has been to pursue success in management from an intellectual standpoint, devising scientific theories from which 'the very latest' systems can be applied. By way of such alchemy we have the bureaucracy of performance appraisal, the mechanics of management by objectives and the rigidity of briefing groups. Reliance is placed on logical processes such as diagnosis, analysis, cost-evaluation and trendy formulae for projecting success.

While intelligence and its resulting pseudo-scientific management approach is highly valued, convention has it that there is little place for emotion in management. Emotion is considered dangerous and a potential threat. Negative emotions can indeed be exceptionally dangerous.

However in sustaining the integrity of an organization there is an essential place for positive emotion. Passion, enthusiasm and excitement are but three emotional facets of leadership that have received scant study over recent times. Without such emotion the integrity of an organization will disintegrate.

> 'We have a boss who is exceptionally nice as long as we do what he wants. But he sulks if we don't. He doesn't like it when we disagree with him. He doesn't tell us what he really thinks, he just goes miserable. He's not honest with us, he's not straight-up. We have to guess at what he thinks by judging his mood. We all find it a bit unsettling at times.
>
> 'He's no comparison with our previous boss. Whatever the occasion you'd walk away from her feeling pretty good, feeling that she'd listened and really understood. What's more she made you feel important. Her enthusiasm for us, for our team, for our company was infectious.
>
> 'We had such a good spirit then. It's gone now.'

In my view the inspirational and intuitive leader has the capability of injecting emotional energies into the otherwise dry mechanistic processes of management. To achieve a vision of success a team needs to become alive with passion, enthusiasm and excitement. Such vitality can never be dispensed through the dreadfully boring bureaucracy of performance appraisal, management by objectives and team briefing.

In terms of integrity, emotion is the binding force which keeps an organization whole.

2

The art of listening and valuing

'A well-trained ear has more value than an active mouth.'

'I find it demoralizing. The directors make the decisions I believe I should be making. I've got specialist knowledge, that's what they employ me for, I think I know what's going on and that I've got something to offer. But I go along to these meetings with directors to impart my knowledge and advice only to find they've made a decision already on my subject and I'm there to be told what to do. Invariably it's a bad decision. They won't listen. It takes weeks if not months to manoeuvre them through a face-saving process to get them to change their mind.'

Some incompetent bosses rarely listen, they deceive themselves they know all the answers, that they know better than their people. Other incompetent bosses listen too much, trying to achieve a consensus when none is possible. As a result decisions get delayed.

Then there are those incompetent bosses who develop delusions that their people are trying to score points, trying to get their own way, are riding hobby-horses, are forever complaining. Some tend to believe that their people don't understand, are not to be trusted and have no worth-while suggestions to make.

Listening is a skill which credible managers develop to a fine art. It reflects a basic attitude by which most people's intrinsic goodwill towards their organization is valued. Most people want their company to do well and want bosses who will listen to the ideas they put forward for improvement. Most people do their best for their company and want bosses who will genuinely recognize and appreciate the contribution they make.

Many bosses are too busy apparently to do this, they cram their diaries full of meetings and seem to have little time for their people. Such bosses effectively devalue their people and fail to recognize the immense contribution they can make.

However, as continually stressed in this book, progress is best made by learning from mistakes. The bosses who fail to listen to their people rarely learn. They are reluctant to admit mistakes, reluctant to admit that in many instances their people are wiser than they, have more valuable perceptions of what is going on, and have the ability to suggest solutions to problems.

Credible bosses get the best out of people by helping them become the best. Part of that process is to devote a lot of time exploring with them their ideas, chewing over problems which inhibit them and providing them with the support they need. It requires recognizing each individual as a unique human being with something very special to offer. People soon feel degraded by bosses who devote little time to them and who are not prepared to listen. Such bosses effectively send out signals saying, 'You are not important, you have nothing special to offer, I am too busy for you.'

Most human beings want to be appreciated and require genuine signals from their bosses that this is the case. All too frequently people don't know where they stand with their boss, feel frustrated that 'management' is unaware of what's going on (in other words, what they are thinking and saying).

There is no 'text-book' way for listening and valuing. Part of the art of leadership is to develop the appropriate personal processes and behaviours for this to take place. Credible bosses will decide whether weekly informal team sessions, occasional awaydays or other methods are best for the listening process. They will seek out the best ways of expressing their appreciation of their people; this might include spontaneous gestures such as taking the team out for lunch, a carefully worded letter of thanks or some other approach which will be well-received.

The key in listening and valuing must be to conduct the chosen process in a sincere, genuine and meaningful way. Artificial devices and personnel procedures aimed at getting managers to listen and value their people often dissipate into bureaucratic chores which managers carry out reluctantly and without conviction. When this happens integrity and credibility rapidly become eroded.

> 'My boss is charming, courteous and spends a lot of time with us in meetings. But there are certain issues – like resourcing levels – where he has a blind spot. No matter what we say he just won't listen. Every time we raise these subjects you can see him switching off. I don't think he understands what goes on at shop-floor level. He's got no idea of the pressures we're under and the hours we're putting in.'

The best test of listening is whether a boss follows through on the ideas and suggestions put forward by the team. 'Actions speak louder than words.' Bosses who merely listen but never take action undermine their credibility. All too frequently employees say, 'I mentioned it to the boss three months ago but nothing has happened.'

Credible bosses take care to listen to all their people and take action on what they hear. In that way they value their people's contribution. After all, if their contribution is not valuable why are they there?

3

Perception and self-deception

'We are all too limited to discover the truth at the first attempt.'

When we see something we only see a fraction of what there is to see at that moment. We select what we want to see, filtering out visual data we're not interested in. We see the face but not the wall behind. We see the smile but not the thoughts behind it. Similarly with hearing, we only hear what we want to hear. Background noise is eliminated as we focus our attention on the words. Words we don't like are eliminated as we focus our attention on the words we want to hear.

And having selected what we want to see and hear from the vast amount of information available, we place our own preferred interpretation on the data selected. We process another person's smile through a 'smile processor' in our brain. This will interpret the smile as being false or genuine, ingratiating or sincere. We take the words from the memo and use the 'interpreter' to translate them into something meaningful for us. 'Meaningful' often means 'what we like' or 'what we don't like'.

Such are our perceptions. And our perceptions are extremely limited. They are limited by our own faculties, our brain power, our past experiences, our emotions, our feelings, our likes and dislikes, our motivations, our knowledge, our values and beliefs, our inclinations for survival and success.

In this perceptual processing there is a great tendency for the truth to become distorted such that what is presented to the brain and subsequently re-presented to the outside world is a series of half-truths, delusions, self-deceits and misunderstandings. In more cynical moments one wonders whether the truth will ever be known.

Governments, boards of directors and most of us make judgements based on perceptions rather than facts. Facts which indicate the inadequacy of previous decisions are normally not welcome, being against the interests of decision-makers and their entrenched needs to preserve face. Where politicians lead, others follow. Industry confuses the public and itself by projecting its own self-interested perceptions of what is good for people irrespective of contrary perceptions from independent voices. The food we eat, the water we drink, the air we breathe and the alcohol we indulge in are all subject to a range of conflicting perceptions of how healthy or unhealthy they are. Some would even have us believe that smoking tobacco is not unhealthy. The public is confused if not deceived by governments and boards of directors who deceive themselves with their own self-interested perceptions of the truth. But it is not the truth.

Perceptions and their limitations lead to corruptions. Organizations become corrupt as self-interest bulldozes its way through contradictory facts and shovels out distorted perceptions that this transportation system is safe, that this food is healthy, that this organization places high value on employee communications. In this context only facts which support the perception are relevant. All other facts are irrelevant. Food-labellers are arch-exponents of fact-manipulation to reinforce the desired perception by the consumer. Such manipulative reinforcement is often blatantly deceitful. Just look at the sugar content of many so-called healthy food products. The 'health' connotation will be highlighted in the packaging labelling while the sugar content is virtually hidden.

It takes a great boss, with an immense amount of integrity, to challenge the conventional perceptions of what is best, what is good, what is necessary, and what the organization is all about.

Integrity is easily eroded as others pressure us with their distorted perceptions of the world, perceptions which are often at total variance to our own.

Lesser managers easily succumb, adopting the perceptions of others and ignoring (if not losing) their own. Ignorance and naivety proliferate as a result.

The great leaders are iconoclasts, are heretics who struggle for the truth from within themselves as opposed to those perceived by the world. They become themselves with their own carefully worked through versions of reality rather than purveyors of the world's distorted perceptions of it. Similarly they help their own people discover the same truth from within, protecting them from attempted corruptions from the organization's system.

'I find that many of my colleagues on the board consistently make the assumption that the people down the line are irresponsible, inexperienced, not to be trusted and incapable of making any other than petty decisions.

'I try to explain it's different, but they won't listen and they won't understand. I give my people a lot of licence and they respond magnificently. I don't find they squander company resources – in fact they're more frugal than I am. Our finance director nearly had a heart attack when I informed him about the level of spending decision I had delegated down to branch level. But this year I've had the best results ever.'

The lesson is never to accept one's immediate interpretation of events, nor for that matter that of others either. Competent bosses challenge what they see and hear, challenge their own perceptions as well as those of others. Whether it be an individual's performance, the competition's capability, the power of the trade union, or the service provided from the centre – they will always challenge their own perception of it.

They see this process of challenging perceptions as the only way to access the facts and discover the truth behind the façade of impressions.

Life is a voyage of discovery. The opportunities for success will always exist but can only be seized when you challenge your perception of them.

4

Inner dignity and intrinsic worth

'We all have a psychological skin to protect us from the rough and tumble of verbal jest, off-hand criticism, malicious accusation and inadvertent rejection.

'When the skin is pierced we bleed inside. The intimidation, the abuse, the scorn, the mockery, the humiliation can destroy our innermost sense of dignity.'

> 'I reckon we dehumanize people in this organization, we degrade them. The accepted style now is to thump the table, to make people feel small, to prove that you're cleverer than the person next to you. The more you humiliate the more you achieve, that's the prevailing culture. I'm exaggerating, of course, but it's true. It started when the new chief executive took over. They all copy him, they've become contaminated with it. It impresses some people but I don't know who.'

Without inner dignity no one can perform. Our psychological heart is ripped out. We lose confidence, develop serious self-doubts and recoil into hideous shells manifest often by incomprehensible distortions of attitude and behaviour.

The incredibly good bosses go out of their way to preserve an individual's sense of inner dignity. The incredibly bad bosses just trample over people, destroying their perceived worth.

The skill is to eliminate imperfection and improve performance without destroying dignity. The worst bosses focus only on imperfection, exaggerating it, projecting it as the person. They ignore the essential good and the intrinsic worth of the person. No individual is without worth. Poor bosses have little sense of value and are blind to worth. They see imperfections and therefore people as worthless, as bad. Such bosses live in a constant state of rage, seeing the world, the organization, their teams as a never-ending set of imperfections, of frustrations, of misunderstandings, of inadequacies and poor performance against which they fight all the time.

With their respect for authority and with fear many people come to believe the bad bosses. They become conditioned by their opinions. These people come to believe they are useless, worthless, incompetent, incapable. They come to lose their inner dignity, their sense of value in contributing. Rather than eliminating their imperfections and performing more effectively they lose their nerve, go into shells and perform less well as they attempt to hide their potential imperfections.

With genuine respect the more competent boss values the real worth of each individual in the team. Such bosses reflect each person's intrinsic worth by the trust they place in them, and in doing so they help enhance the self-value felt by each individual. Part of that enhancement process is enabling each person to recognize and eliminate imperfections.

Such improvement enhances the worth in the eyes of the boss and thus the dignity felt by the person. Conversely those bosses who focus only on imperfections as opposed to intrinsic worth and improvement effectively devalue people and erode their inner dignity.

Most people need a lot of help in discovering their real worth. They lose sight of it quickly. We are all subjected to a worldly conditioning process which judges snippets of observed behaviour as totally representative of that person. We become conditioned by the world's perception of us and behave accordingly.

People of stature rise above the world's perception of themselves. Through a lifetime's experience of listening, learning and self-analysis they are constantly making discoveries about their true self. That true self, as it becomes discovered, is immutable and cannot be destroyed by intimidation and organization abuse. This process of discovery provides essential strength to the manager under conflict and pressure, and is critical for high performance.

> 'Throughout my career in this organization I've seen boss after boss take away the dignity from people. They lose their temper, they shout, they put people down. It has appalling consequences. Despite the blurbage coming out from the board we are just not a people-caring organization.'

A successful boss spends a lot of time helping individuals identify and develop the intrinsic worth within their true selves. In doing so he or she enables them to develop their own sense of inner dignity.

Expressed another way, success in management is predominantly a matter of self-belief. Those who allow their inner dignities and self-beliefs to be destroyed by rampant bosses can never succeed. Conversely, excellent bosses go out of their way to develop self-belief and dignity in all members of their team.

5

Hidden agendas and ulterior motivations

'There is nothing so discreditable as ulterior motives.'

Integrity and credibility in management is best achieved when bosses come clean with their motives. Conversely they will demand the same of their people. Uncertainty and poor performance occur when people become suspicious of the motivations of others.

When you don't know what the boss is getting at, you will second-guess and in all probability get it wrong. You will feel unsure. You will deploy your attention away from the main task as you try to work out what he or she really means. Bosses who are not straight, who have hidden agendas, who try to tell you things indirectly, drain their people's interpretive energy.

To achieve the maximum integrity and credibility the greatest task is to examine and be honest about your own motives. It is no easy task when we are all subject to intense selfish drives, when we are all subject to conflicting forces within ourselves. Essential chores are avoided while non-essential trips overseas are presented as essential in the never-ending quest to escape from the drudgery of the office. Extended tea breaks become more important than serving the customer as motivations become entangled in a web of self-preservation, relief and reaction against the bosses who fail to understand. Avoidance behaviour, innuendo and talking behind people's backs become the norm for people who cannot confront their own motives, who seek to fulfil their drives through undisclosed indirect routes.

There is no absolute. Like everything in life there is a spectrum across which we have to find our own balance. The mark of civilization is to control our own selfish motivations which, if uncontrolled, would otherwise destroy the society in which we live.

We might be motivated to obtain promotion but consistently declaring that motive might well destroy promotion prospects as senior bosses perceive too much self-interest and aggrandizement on display. So we pretend not to be interested in promotion while in fact we are and our behaviours indirectly show this.

Motives can soon turn into obsessions. In the work place the reality is that we are paid to be motivated to achieve specified organization goals. Personal motivations, such as overseas travel, promotion, resting, chatting to people we like, often interfere with the 'paid for' motivation. It is difficult to admit our preference for chatting up an attractive person when those miserable people in accounts require priority attention.

Superbosses have the wisdom to identify motivations within themselves which have to be eliminated. They then eliminate them, rather than seek indirect outlets for them. They become adept at filtering out all these extraneous motivations which interfere with the achievement of their main goal. In doing so they are able to concentrate their motivational energies in contributing to the organization; and in doing so they have no problem in being totally open and honest about their motivations – because there are no ulterior motives. Their personal behaviours reflect this. With such an approach there is no diffusion of energies into avoidance behaviours, into innuendo and other alienating behaviours. Hidden agendas are out because nothing is hidden.

Consequently the whole team is able to understand clearly the motivations behind the boss's behaviour.

Your test today and every day, as a boss, is to relate clearly all your behaviours to your motives and ensure that your people understand them.

If the motive behind your behaviour is not apparent to you, then it will not be to the people in your team. Performance will deteriorate accordingly.

6

From frustration to inspiration

'To succeed a boss has to rise above all those dreary frustrating mechanisms of management.'

Success can never be achieved through a process of bureaucracy. The more forms to be filled in, the more reports to be written, the more controls to be exercised the more frustrating the task of management will become and the more elusive success will be.

Procedures, manuals, policies and departmental notices serve only to constrain and limit the freedom of those who might otherwise, given a freer hand, succeed on behalf of the organization.

To succeed people need to feel excited, need to feel good. They need to enjoy those 'highs' which are experienced when people approach and achieve success. They need to feel the elation of having to face up to an incredible challenge. They need to thrill to the demand from their boss for a unique contribution from them.

To succeed people need inspiration.

Short-term success can be achieved by logic and analysis. But long-term success can only be achieved by inspirational bosses who excite their teams with major challenges.

Such inspirational bosses inject positive emotion into their business dream and articulate that dream in clear simple terms which

84

have dramatic personal meaning for every single individual in the team.

Inspiration is the process of stimulating a team, invigorating them, giving them total energy – emotional, spiritual, intellectual and physical. It is the process of arousing a team to the exciting possibilities of even greater levels of performance and success.

Without inspiration bosses become administrators and controllers. They become a drag on the organization with their monotonous paper-led routines of minuted meetings and hideous agendas. Without inspiration bosses turn people off, inadvertently injecting drudgery and boredom into a mechanistic process of bureaucratically formulated organization aims, objectives and controls.

Without inspiration bosses drift into a lament of disinterest. They become uninteresting people, preoccupied only with rules and regulations as an establishment of their own power and status. They fear excitement, passion, stimulation, invigoration and inspiration – perceiving such emotion as a threat with the potential to unleash human forces they cannot control. So they seek to dampen such forces by spraying down their teams with paper.

Those superbosses who lead to succeed set out to inspire their teams. They seek to share with their team the excitement of meeting the great challenges in front of them. They seek to get the whole team vibrant with such positive energy that they feel they can climb unclimbable mountains.

'Someone has to be the best in this area. Why not us?' is the challenge the inspirational boss lays before his or her team. 'Why should we aim to be second best? Why should we be ordinary? Why should we drift into the mediocrity we see in others? Don't we want to be the best? Don't we want to be unique? Don't we want to be leading the way? Most importantly don't we owe it to our customers to give them of our best? If we don't succeed in this, others will!'

Organization constraints exist everywhere, they never go away and even competitors have them! In fact an organization without constraint would be an organization verging on anarchy. The worst bosses hide behind these constraints, blame them, use them as an excuse for non-achievement. The incredibly successful bosses make things happen whatever the level of constraint. Their teams achieve what others consider impossible. They get the resources others are denied, they get the support so easily withdrawn from weaker brethren, they get their way when lesser brethren find the same way blocked. Their energy, their dedication, their commitment, their belief becomes infectious. They infect the hierarchy, through a process of persistent persuasion, influence and inspiration to endorse their vision and their way. Others might perceive it as single-mindedness, ruthlessness if not pig-headedness.

Inspiration comes from a genuine belief that you can succeed despite all the alleged limitations, despite all the assertions that you cannot succeed. Without limitation there would be no success. Success is all about exceeding limits.

Business history is full of stories of those who have defied the constraints with which others seek to limit them.

The impossible can never be attained, but the near-impossible can. It requires the inspiration drawn from the belief that nearly everything one dreams of in life is virtually achievable. It is a belief that life is full of opportunity. There is only one constraint, and that is the person perceiving it. The opportunity which you are constrained from seizing will *always* be seized by someone else.

Inspiration is the process of shedding these constraints and discovering the energy to seize and realize opportunity. In that way even you can get to the moon!

7

Converting weaknesses to strengths

'Credibility can never be achieved by suppressing weaknesses. Humility is a key to credibility.'

We wish to enhance our credibility in the eyes of others by appearing important, knowledgeable and successful. Acknowledging our many imperfections and mistakes appears to diminish our importance, our knowledge and our success. But it doesn't, that's the paradox. Humility is essential in achieving high credibility.

We fear being discredited in the eyes of others. So we suppress our weaknesses. We hide them from our bosses knowing they will penalize us with poor pay increases and no promotion if we appear weak.

We do not learn. We do not learn that only by exposing our weaknesses do we learn. We do not learn that the continued promotion and exhibition of our strengths (glory-seeking) will reduce our credibility rather than enhance it.

Those who seek credibility never attain it. Credibility is conferred on individuals by others. To achieve credibility one cannot market oneself by highlighting strengths and projecting oneself in the best light. Short-term positive impressions might be obtained, as at an interview, but in the long term the real person will show through – and credibility is only conferred on real people, not on impressions obtained.

Strength comes from admitting weaknesses, exposing them to those trusted people who can provide counsel and positive support. Ideally that person is the boss who needs, for the sake of the organization, to help you grow strong from identifying and eliminating weaknesses.

Suppressing weaknesses further weakens the person and the organization.

Incredibly many senior executives create cultures where the suppression of weakness prevails. Despite performance appraisal systems they attempt to motivate through 'carrot and stick' which paradoxically mitigates against the exposure of weaknesses. People put a gloss on their performance to enhance pay and promotion prospects, weaknesses are suppressed.

It takes a tolerant and understanding boss to accept the weaknesses of his team. It takes a patient and persevering boss to sit down with team-members and help them eradicate these weaknesses and make improvements. Far easier to ignore these weaknesses and then finally, when it comes to the crunch, fire the people exhibiting them.

The superboss seeks not to fire, nor to expose weaknesses but to help individuals improve. People know this and volunteer their weaknesses as part of the improvement process, aware that the boss will not penalize them for such personal honesty.

> 'I'll tell you about my boss, he's got a long successful career in paranoia. He's out to prove that the world, the organization, his own boss and us in the team are against him.
>
> 'The trouble is he's probably right!'

If, as a last resort both boss and team-member agree that the weakness is impossible to eradicate and that it impedes the achievement of the boss's vision then the decision is obvious. The person would be better suited to another job.

In the ideal world it should be as above. Occasionally weaknesses are so suppressed that a person will never own up to them. In these situations disagreements and confrontations will inevitably arise. Credible bosses have the courage to confront the resulting conflict. Ultimately if the weakness is so damaging and so suppressed that the person won't own up to it, then he or she will have to be dismissed.

Even so, before superbosses act upon the weaknesses of others they look carefully at their own and act upon these. This can be a more productive area for organization improvement than any other.

The best boss is one who encourages the team to expose their real weaknesses.

8

The uncertainty factor

'Nothing destroys morale and reduces performance more than uncertainty.'

If you are certain your boss has no scruples then you can adjust accordingly and perform quite well.

If you are uncertain how your boss will behave then you will work in fear, forever unsure of his reaction to your efforts, forever unsure as to whether you're in for praise, a reprimand or nothing at all.

People who are uncertain whether their unit will be axed will perform less effectively than those who feel secure in their jobs.

The credible boss creates a climate of certainty. People will feel secure with him or her, know where they are. They are certain that they will get praise when it's due and a reprimand if deserved. They are certain that their boss will devote time to them and come round and see them on a regular basis.

Performance suffers when you're never sure; when you're unsure if your boss is going to catch you out, or criticize you for making a decision, or slap you down in front of others, or send you yet another stroppy memo, or demand more information, or hijack your meetings schedule, or refuse your requests for a day off. Unpredictability can be a nightmare.

There is nothing wrong with the occasional spontaneous gesture (bringing in doughnuts for the team) but to trade on people's uncertainty can be highly dangerous and erode credibility.

People get distracted, gossiping and guessing what will happen next. Output suffers.

Far better to be open and honest, to flush out doubts, reduce uncertainty as far as possible and then let people get on with the job.

> **'After months of rumours and speculation the company finally announced it was going to relocate its head office. We all became a bit unsettled wondering whether we'd be keeping our jobs or not. When the announcement was made the chief executive promised we'd all know within two weeks what was going to happen to us individually. That was eight weeks ago. We've heard nothing since then. Nobody seems to know what's going on. I've covered my options. I've got an interview with another company next week.'**

Sometimes uncertainty is inevitable, for example whether or not the company is going to secure a major contract. But other times uncertainty is avoidable. The incredibly poor bosses neglect to inform, keep people waiting, create uncertainty of the highest level.

Managerial competence and credibility is very much dependent on establishing secure relationships with subordinates based on a high degree of 'certainty' of behaviour.

9

Selfish needs

'The selfish bosses are those who value themselves more than their people.'

We all have needs. We become selfish when we put these needs before those of others. Many managers do so often and as such they lose credibility and perform badly.

At one level convention has it that the needs of shareholders are put before those of employees. Such prioritization carries little weight in the study of success. At another level selfish bosses pursue only those matters of interest to themselves, neglecting to address issues of interest to their people. As a result their people develop resentments about their bosses disregard of their own needs. Such neglect is often shown through inadequate communication, a lack of involvement, failure to recognize and appreciate good work, and a reluctance to delegate and trust. All bosses do, in the pursuit of their selfish needs, is place demands on their people, whose needs regarding working conditions, tools for their jobs, training as well as direct participation in the future success of the organization go unheeded.

- The director travels first-class, his or her managers don't. Why?

- The managers have the freedom to entertain business visitors but their people don't. Why?

- The supervisors are allowed extended lunch-breaks, but their people aren't. Why?

There are numerous other examples. It is easy to rationalize and argue that if such freedoms were delegated to the lowest levels there would be anarchy. Indeed there would be in an organization lacking in trust and integrity, in an organization which had lost all credibility with its employees.

But the real reasons are far removed from the falsity of those stated. The real reason is the selfish needs of those bosses for the trappings of power, the manifestations of status and the pursuit of self-esteem. Weak bosses like to feel important, like to have people running round after them, like to be treated like royalty. They like to have people at their beck and call, like to have people 'sucking up' to them. They genuinely believe that the trappings of status confer credibility in the eyes of all.

They like travelling first-class, it makes them feel important, and feeling important is a selfish need. They will argue that their time is precious and first-class travel enables them to work on the train or the plane. But the same applies to more junior staff. The sacrifices junior staff make working excessively long hours are such that anyone working long hours should travel first-class on business. In that way the organization could openly and honestly acknowledge all of our needs for comfort, for feeling important, for working effectively. The impact on motivation and consequently competent performance would be dramatic. Profits would increase!

> 'Our previous boss was great, he gave us time. You could take your problems to him, he would listen, he would understand, he would help. Then he retired and they brought in this new whiz-kid. We never see him, you can never get in to talk to him, he's never around. He only seems to work for himself, not for us. It's not surprising profits have gone down since he's been on board.'

One cannot escape selfish needs. It is only when they are openly and honestly acknowledged and addressed that any conflict between them can be reduced and integrity and credibility is achieved.

Meeting everyone's needs, however, is an ideal. The credible bosses therefore go out of their way to meet the needs of their people before those of their own.

10

Indirect signals

'The indirect often undermines the direct.'

Indirect signals come thick and fast in most organizations. People don't call back, that's an indirect signal. Others don't get invited to meetings when they think they should, another signal. Others don't get told about anything. Memos get sent which you have to read between the lines to understand. Poor performers are left on the by-line and imagine they're performing well. High-flyers are given a 'nod and wink' that they are being groomed for stardom. These are all indirect signals. Whom the boss lunches with is a signal. Whom the boss talks to informally is a signal.

The reality is we give off signals all the time. A smile or lack of smile is a signal. The way we answer the telephone is a signal. The worst bosses avoid direct communication and create, by default, a vacuum of indirect signals which the team with their sensitive antennae go to great lengths to interpret and under-stand. Inevitably these interpretations are often wrong and lead to misunderstandings which drain an organization of morale.

To achieve integrity excellent bosses minimize the risk of indirect signals sparking unnecessary problems and place great emphasis on frequent and direct honest communication.

They are exceptionally sensitive to how people might interpret the signals they emit. Their strategy therefore is to create a climate of trust whereby any indirect signals are of low intensity and perceived as insignificant. Such a climate can only be achieved by frequent two-way communication in which everyone is encouraged to speak about their thoughts and feelings on a range of issues, in which everyone is encouraged to raise any misunderstanding and question their interpretation of behaviours by others.

'My boss has been around a long time. He makes it 100 per cent clear he doesn't approve of this new director they've just brought in. In fact my boss just radiates cynicism every time you mention this new director's name or mention some of the exciting ideas he's trying to introduce. At our management meeting I tried to get a debate going on one or two of these ideas. Without doing it directly my boss just poured cold water on it all, implying this new director didn't understand the realities of the business.'

By achieving total trust within the group the leader establishes an expectation that anything of importance will be communicated directly. It is when there is a lack of trust, and low integrity, that people place more reliance on indirect signals to interpret their fates.

To achieve integrity and high credibility the indirect signals must be totally consistent with the direct signals.

11

Stereotyping

'Stereotyping short-circuits deep thinking.'

- He's a 'nine-to-fiver'.
- She's a 'pain-in-the-neck'.
- He's a typical finance guy, only thinks money.
- She's a whiz-kid.

People are incredibly complex, so complex in fact that we cannot comprehend them in our simple little minds!

So we stereotype them, extracting one or two blatant characteristics to sort them into stereotypical boxes.

The process is akin to prejudice.

It's our lack of ability to see and understand everything about a person. So rather than try to see more and understand more, which the best bosses do, we make premature judgements based on fragmented perceptions which fit comfortably into these stereotypical boxes.

It short-circuits that difficult and uncertain process of getting all the information we need before making a judgement about a person. By stereotyping people we can make instant decisions about them. We think we know how the stereotype is going to behave, what their attitudes, beliefs and commitment will be. It's all there in the box for us to see, a box based on ill-digested experiences and insufficient challenge. It's a box which forecasts behaviour and becomes a self-fulfilling prophecy in that it excludes behaviours which do not fit in and only accepts behaviours which do. When we see a stereotype behaving in a non-stereotype way we reject or ignore the observation, finding it irrelevant in the judgemental process. Stereotyping induces blindness in managers, reducing their credibility as they rush into prejudicial judgements. 'She's a typical personnel type.' 'He's a wheeler-dealer.'

In the work-place there are many stereotypes, for example: the sales rep, the trade union official, the internal auditor, the English expatriate, the old bore, the 'old woman', the 'yes-man' and the feminist. All are based on distorted images and perceptions.

Stereotyping belies integrity and diminishes credibility all around. It by-passes that essential process of discovering the fascinating truth about people. It leads dangerously to biased and prejudicial decisions. 'All Indians smell of curry.' 'All black people are noisy.' 'All women are emotional.' 'All Englishmen are reserved.'

'When I joined I was treated as the lowest of the low. I had to make the coffee, I had to go and get the rolls for everyone else at break-time, I had to go and get stationery from the stores. Then a new boss arrived. The second day he brought me coffee. Come Friday he took us all out for a drink at lunch time. I couldn't believe it. I'd never realized bosses were human beings!'

Stereotyping is endemic in the fast-moving commercial world where people don't have time to think. Stereotyping is an immense threat to integrity and is an attribute of incredibly incompetent bosses.

Successful bosses take care not to rush into premature judgements about people. They avoid the glib use of stereotypical descriptions and, more importantly, avoid making decisions based on them.

12

Subjective assessment

'Our feelings about individuals can change from hour to hour and this affects our judgement in the management process.'

One minute we feel angry with our kids, they're so noisy, so untidy. The next minute they're pandering to our whims with token efforts to tidy up and we think they're wonderful. The same with our partners, sometimes they get on our nerves, other times it's heaven to be with them.

And with bosses too, and subordinates. We can irritate them, we can please them. We can be petty, we can be easy-going, depending on our mood.

When one moment you feel good about a person and the next you feel bad it's difficult to assess that person objectively. Subjectivity looms large in most assessment processes, despite attempts to be objective.

The text-books say you should set objectives and measure performance against them. But it's never as easy as that because the interpretation of capability and achievement will depend on how you feel about the person. And when your feelings vary from time to time it's difficult to arrive at a firm assessment on which you feel confident.

A boss can sit down to prepare a performance appraisal only to find that, when the person walks smiling through the door and begins to expound on her successes, the perception changes, the assessment changes and the preparation goes out of the window.

Certain people are very plausible in face-to-face encounters yet when they are seen from a distance they appear less plausible.

Changing perceptions, subjective judgements and variable assessments lead to an erosion of a boss's credibility and integrity. A boss might believe a person has performance limitations one minute and the next minute advise that person that he or she is doing exceptionally well. But he or she will know. People have very sensitive antennae and realize when a boss is putting a gloss on the assessment or playing down any reservations.

You can never be sure. Unless you are completely honest with yourself and the other person. This requires careful identification of all subjective factors including likes and dislikes in an attempt to improve the objectivity of assessment. What you daren't do is ignore these factors. To achieve credibility and integrity you cannot discard subjective factors and pretend you are concentrating only on objective ones. If you do so your assessment will be distorted, lop-sided and misleading.

By allowing subjective factors to come to the surface you can objectively discuss them with the other person and assess their impact (if any) on performance.

It requires clear thinking and a clear understanding of a certain management fundamental – that subjectivity is as inescapable as the honest truth.

If you attempt to ignore your likes and dislikes about a person you will inadvertently rationalize your decisions in attempting to be objective. Far better to come clean with the person and acknowledge the dislikes and then examine carefully whether they have a direct or indirect impact on performance. If they do, you should constructively advise the person being assessed.

The complication is, as mentioned at the outset, that we tend to have both likes and dislikes for one person, and these likes and dislikes never come to the fore at the same time. Many people being assessed manipulate the assessment by simulating a range of sophisticated 'likeable' behaviours (forever agreeing, forever appearing willing).

> 'We worked all weekend on that urgent export order. I personally cancelled a family outing to help the firm out, to ensure we met the deadline. But we didn't see our boss that weekend at all. He didn't even put an appearance in. Come Monday morning we didn't see him either, he didn't even bother to come down and say "thank you". Tuesday morning I was twenty minutes late because I had to take my daughter to hospital. He called me in and gave me a right going over for being late.'

As a test, spend some time considering your most senior subordinates and list down your likes and dislikes of them. Now be honest and analyse carefully how these likes and dislikes influence your assessment of each person's performance. Now compare the result with what you last wrote down on the assessment form.

You cannot avoid subjectivity in a management assessment process, so be honest about it.

13

Personality clashes

'Personalities often clash when people are not open and honest about their likes and dislikes for each other.'

There is a myth that the process of management is an objective one, that there is no place for 'personality' in such a process.

Conversely there is another myth that there are 'appropriate' personalities for certain jobs and what you need to do is measure and profile the personality, testing it to help identify the right person for the job. Managers become seduced by psychologists who fail to advise them on the difference between personality, skill, attitude and experience.

The reality is that personality does have a major impact on job performance. However, the process of assessing personality and relating it to competence is essentially a subjective one, the main reason being that one's perception of competence is frequently clouded by personal likenesses, affinities, comfort levels, attractions and shared interests. Personality is essentially a function of relationships and trying to measure it individually in isolation from others is foolhardy.

With rare exceptions high performance is dependent on successful relationships. To perform excellently everyone needs someone else. Relationship needs are best met when you like the people you work with as well as your boss, are comfortable with them, have common values and beliefs, share many interests and have mutual respect. These are all subjective factors for which there are often no rational explanations (in the same way that there is no simple rationale for the attraction between a man and a woman). Thus there is no simple logic which can explain why a new recruit will or will not fit effectively into a team.

Scientific management demands that these subjective elements are either suppressed or eliminated, objectivity being a prized value.

Recognition of personality as a key subjective element in relationships and therefore performance is vital in the pursuit of managerial competence. To rationalize personality differences through a process of simulated objectivity is an erosion of integrity and will diminish credibility.

Personality clashes can best be resolved by addressing the subjective factors (e.g. emotions and feelings) rather than resorting to faked objectivity.

> 'Every quarter we have this regional meeting. Sometimes our director brings along the marketing director to take our questions on marketing. We know they don't get on well together. So we deliberately lob controversial questions into them and then stand back waiting for the fireworks. Invariably there's a major argument between the two as they fight it out in public. It's all a game really. It's amazing!'

The resolution of a personality clash requires an honest analysis of why each party 'dislikes' the other. If that process is handled in a way that each party can discuss his or her dislike of the other, with the other, then there is a high probability that those 'dislikes' and the resultant clashes will disappear – especially if there is a discovery of likes previously hidden. Counselling is often required to facilitate this delicate process. A wise boss, sensing a personality clash, will carefully choose someone all parties will trust to undertake such counselling.

To achieve credibility a boss must be open and honest in acknowledging the subjective nature of personality and its influence on relationships and thus performance.

14

Passive resistance

'Why risk getting fired with open and active dissent when you can passively resist?

'It needs guts to speak up to an alien boss.'

> 'In our department people aren't given praise. The boss never comes along and says "That piece of work was good". He never demonstrates gratitude or appreciation. We just think he takes us for granted. So we take him for a ride now, pretending to work hard when he's around and taking it easy when he's not.'

In the absence of guts there is indirect dissent, a passive resistance of insubordination, excuses and delays. People keep their eyes down when the boss walks in. People stare at the window when the boss asks for volunteers. People raise their eyebrows when the boss makes statements they disagree with. People go into corners and sulk. They go slow.

Customers don't get served when there's gossip behind closed doors. Little gets followed through, in-trays pile up. Telephones aren't answered. Problems are never owned up to.

It's normally the boss's fault. It always is. He or she has switched off the team, precipitated them into a mode of passive resistance. The boss has probably humiliated one or all of them from time to time, has alienated them with his or her inconsiderate ways, has unfairly disciplined people when things haven't happened. The boss never recognizes the hard work people put in, never bothers to say 'thank you'. He or she never listens, never finds time for them. Now they don't bother, now they don't care. They give as good as they take, ignoring her, avoiding him.

Passive resistance occurs when bosses become immersed in their own thing. Preoccupied with their own selfish goals, they discount the role of others which they perceive as detracting from their mission. They believe they fight a lone battle. They do but engender passive resistance in the process.

> 'In four years I've had no support at all from my boss, no feedback at all. I make up my own mind how well I'm doing. He is very cold, he never talks with me. The most you get is instructions. He does it to my staff too. We just ignore him. I know what I want and so do my staff. They tell me what they think about him.'

There is no integrity nor credibility when you are only interested in yourself or your narrow perception of what the company wants. Your self-centred approach reduces your own credibility and precipitates people into resistant behaviours which they themselves dislike and which threaten their own integrity.

People like to get their own way and resent bosses alone getting theirs. Passive resistance is the result.

> 'It's got so bad here people won't speak up at meetings. They listen blankly to what the bosses have to say, then rubbish their decisions as soon as they are outside the door. It's pure passive resistance. It's endemic in the company. I don't suppose the bosses even know.'

Superbosses free people, enabling them to get their own way whenever they can, knowing that people rarely abuse the freedoms given them, knowing that their own way is often best. Occasionally they will decide against that way taking care to explain that there is a better approach. In a climate of trust and respect people will accept his or her decision.

When integrity and trust exist between a boss and the team there is a greater probability that everyone will get their own way, without conflict or passive resistance, in achieving great results.

15

Fear of owning up

'In fearing a loss of credibility by owning up, people lose further credibility by covering up.'

People are frail. Their weaknesses show up in the mistakes they make. These mistakes often rebound on the organization they work for, if not the public at large.

They get blamed, vilified. The evidence is for all to see – 'AIR-LINE PILOT BLAMED FOR CRASH'. So in fear of humiliation people cover up. A water-authority accidentally leaks poison into a river. It fears owning up, it covers up. An airplane manufacturer discovers faulty wiring on a number of its jet-liners but fails to tell the aviation authority for five months. It fears owning up, it covers up.

The conventional but deceptive wisdom is that exposure of mistakes discredits people. The unbelievable truth is that the converse is true. It is the cover-up that discredits people, that diminishes the belief in those attempting to hide something.

To own up to a mistake actually enhances credibility. Furthermore, it enables the owner to learn, to avoid repeating the mistake. People who cover up eventually delude themselves, through a complex psychological process, that they never made the mistake in the first place. They never learn. They become incompetent.

The process of 'owning up' can be painful. But it is less painful than having your cover-up uncovered. The truth is it was your mistake. It was your calamity. You caused the disaster. The mistake will lie with you even if you won't admit it to others let alone yourself. And as long as it lies with you, suppressed and covered up it will affect you adversely. You will fear it. Your competence and credibility will suffer. In the end you will avoid your conscience because your conscience tells you it was your mistake.

The only way to alleviate a mistake is to expose it, discuss it and learn from it. First of all you have to expose it to yourself and then, when you have the courage, expose it to others including your boss. If your boss is wild enough to punish you for your mistake then so be it, perhaps it's best you don't work for such a wild organization.

'He took us away for an awayday. He'd been our boss for a year now. He said we needed some team-building. On starting the meeting he told us he wanted some feedback, that he wanted us to be open and honest with him. At an opportune moment we raised the issue of our monthly team meetings and what a shambles they were. We rarely saw the agenda before the meeting and the meetings were always being interrupted. He constantly drifted in and out and readily accepted interruptions. Sometimes junior managers were invited to attend part of the meeting to make reports. In one case a manager had to wait four hours outside before we came to his item on the agenda. These meetings invariably drag on.

'His response to this feedback was amazing. He accused us of getting at him, of being racially prejudiced (he was black) and that we were ganging up on him.

'When we tried to explain politely that there was a genuine issue he lost his temper and stormed out of the room.

'Never ever will I go to an awayday again.'

Society is rarely compassionate and rarely tolerant of the failings of others. Such lack leads to the generation of a climate in which bosses, incredibly, go against their instincts for honesty and openness. A climate evolves in which everyone covers up. It's a climate which destroys the credibility and integrity of the organization and most people working within it. In trying to retain credibility by covering up they lose it.

You have nothing to fear but yourself in covering up. You can lose that fear by owning up to your mistakes.

16

Protection mechanisms

'You lose a lot when you force people into self-protection. Performance deteriorates as they protect their pay, protect their jobs, protect their faces, protect decisions already made.'

Reduce the need for self-protection and a person will thrive, no longer fearing the exposure of his or her vulnerabilities and doubts or the consequential abuse. Confidence rarely derives from self-protection, yet confidence coupled with humility is required for the best performance. It is the confidence to have your mistakes and imperfections exposed in order to learn from them. It is the confidence to take risks, to take initiatives and to innovate. It is the confidence that your boss will be supportive rather than punitive.

Superbosses generate high levels of performance from their people by injecting genuine confidence into them. Incredibly bad bosses drain their people of confidence, exposing their inevitable weaknesses in a destructive way which forces them to develop all manner of protection mechanisms.

Protection comes from the union, from the group, from saying nothing, from lying, from hiding, from keeping your head down, from evasive action, from pretence.

As always there is no absolute. You have to take a position on the spectrum between two extremes. People need to protect themselves from their own excesses (smoking, over-eating). People need to wear clothes as well as dress well to protect themselves from abuse or rejection. They need to wear cosmetics to present themselves in the best light. They need the world to see them slightly better than they are in order to protect their inner dignities.

People want protection from bad impressions. So they create artificially good impressions as a protection mechanism. Such are the cosmetics of working life.

The competent boss helps people protect themselves from within rather than by using protective ploys. To protect them directly can be dangerous, leading to paternalism, dependency and a perception that the boss knows better than his or her people. Far better to help people protect themselves by helping them overcome their vulnerabilities and doubts in the search for and discovery of their own truly innate worth. Everyone has such worth.

It takes patience, time, tolerance and empathy to identify your own weaknesses and furthermore to observe similar weaknesses in other human beings. In other people's potential you see your own.

It takes skill to avoid having your behaviours, words, signals and actions misinterpreted by others as threats and abuse. It takes skill to avoid other people developing protection mechanisms against such inadvertent and possibly misconstrued behaviour.

'I avoid my boss like the plague. He's always finding fault, always shouting at people. In the early days I would ask his permission for things, never once did he say "yes". Now I don't ask him and just get on and do things. He's the worst boss I've ever come across. If I hadn't taken out this heavy mortgage I'd leave now.'

Contrary to the myth about macho whiz-kids, about hard-nosed, ruthless, single-minded entrepreneurs, the best bosses are incredibly sensitive towards their people and their need for inner protection.

Sensitivity generates understanding and high performance. It doesn't mean cushioning a person from the truth – but rather exposing the truth in a sensitive way to protect the person from losing face.

17

Problem avoidance

'The incredibly bad bosses develop jungle-like skills in avoiding problems. If only they'd apply these skills to solving these problems they'd be incredibly good bosses.'

> 'My boss doesn't like making difficult decisions. I go to see her and her standard response is "Write me a paper". It's her way of stalling. I write the paper. She sits on it – the average is four weeks. Then she writes back with queries. I write back. Four weeks later she writes back with objections.
>
> 'I don't bother now. I just make the decisions myself and wait for her to catch up with me. She doesn't. She doesn't know the half of what is going on.
>
> 'By comparison when my people come to see me with difficult decisions I discuss these with them fully, perhaps consult one or two people the same day and then make a decision. I know I make mistakes sometimes but my boss never catches me out.'

While most people revel in problems, love identifying them, enjoy nothing more than moaning and groaning about them, few have the courage to solve them. The problem with solving problems is that you suddenly discover that few people accept the solution. It's easy enough for people to point out the problem. But to get people to agree to a solution (let alone propose one) is sometimes nigh impossible.

Delaying tactics, setting up working groups, asking for detailed reports, making excuses about urgent tasks are all methods bosses without integrity use to avoid problems. Somehow they hope the problem will go away. It never does. Invariably it gets worse.

Some problems fester over years, nobody is ever prepared to make a decision. For example, discarding an outmoded and creaking pay-grade structure. Patchwork is done on a month-by-month basis to respond to urgent requirements – but that just makes the long-term problem of inequitable gradings worse.

Another example is tackling restrictive union practices. For many weaker-minded bosses it is easier to live with the problem of gross inefficiency than tackle it. Such bosses (and the trade unions who connive at such bad practice) merely stick their heads in the sand.

Incredibly good bosses 'own' the problem. By identifying a problem that gets in the way of what they want to achieve they accept ownership of the problem. And that means accepting accountability for solving it. Shunting the problem aside and asking other people to solve it for them (for example personnel departments) rarely guarantees success. The best way to solve a problem is to get it solved yourself. It means getting support for the solution from people outside your direct control – an essential part of the problem-solving process which lesser managers shy away from.

For example, if, as an up-and-coming manager, you really believe you have a customer-care problem in your area of responsibility, then you should do battle right through the organization to achieve your end. It's your problem, not that of your boss who doesn't share it, nor that of the directors who have other things on their minds. The problem of an unsympathetic hierarchy and alien organization becomes your problem. You must have the courage to confront that problem. It might mean risking your job, but to solve major problems it's sometimes necessary to put your job on the line.

The biggest problem avoidance area relates to personal issues. Few bosses like dealing with problem people. Frequently they

avoid the problem by re-organizing or simply ignoring the problem. Highly competent bosses never avoid such personal issues.
They confront the problem, tell the individual what they think –
albeit in a constructive and helpful way. To avoid expressing
concern about an individual will erode your integrity. People
will see your avoidance as such, they will see that you are not
prepared to be open and honest with them. Your credibility
suffers as the problem fails to get solved and overall performance
declines.

Another method of problem avoidance is to refuse to accept that
there is a problem. When weak bosses are told that morale is low
in their organization they dismiss the evidence as atypical,
unsymptomatic. They come up with their own anecdotes to
demonstrate the reverse is true. 'Our worsening retention rate
has little to do with low morale,' they will say. 'It's merely a
reflection of increasing competitive pressures in the market
place. It's about time Personnel got their finger out and sorted
the problem.'

Blaming others, making excuses, dismissing the evidence, dis-
crediting the bearer of bad news are all ploys to avoid accepting
the problem. In some organizations problems bounce around
from one 'refusenik' to another, each refusing ownership of the
problem. Sooner or later the problem blows back in the
organization's face to the detriment of all. The workers go on
strike, the professionals leave in droves, the volume of customer
complaints escalate. Profit performance declines dramatically.

> 'Last September our boss told us there would be an organization
> review around December time, but we weren't to worry, our jobs
> would be secure. Come April we had heard nothing. We'd given up
> asking our boss because he just wouldn't give us a straight answer.
> The shock came when four of us saw our own jobs advertised in a
> national newspaper. Nobody had had the courtesy to tell us.
> Apparently we're all being downgraded and will report into these new
> people. It's atrocious!'

No problem is too small for excellent bosses. They realize that a small problem solved today prevents a huge problem tomorrow. The worst bosses don't have time for the small problems and then avoid them when they become too big.

So next time you identify a problem inhibiting the achievement of your vision of success say to yourself, 'It's my problem. I won't thrust it on to my boss or personnel, or a working party. Nor will I ask for a report or allow the problem to sit at the bottom of my in-tray. It's my problem and I'll do something positive today about solving it.'

If you see it as a problem, it's your problem.

18

Rationalization

'Without reason you rationalize.'

The delusion is that you become credible by inventing acceptable reasons, after the event, after the decision. Lack of understanding creates discomfort, so managers obviate the discomfort by creating synthetic understanding. Or deliberate misunderstanding. A plausible reason, invented to impress, appears more acceptable than the unknown real reason. Post-justification becomes the essential norm, everything happening being justified after the event.

There are always reasons why the engineers go on strike, but the stated reasons are totally divorced from the real reasons. When the chief executive resigns, the reasons she states to her team are different from the reasons given in the press announcement, and all these are different from the reasons discussed with the chairman which are again different from the real reasons which neither will admit to themselves.

Rationalization is akin to cover-up. It covers up, even suppresses the real reasons. Rationalization is akin to lying. You invent the story behind the incident to achieve credibility, to prevent the other person thinking less of you.

You dismiss your assistant manager because 'of the need to streamline the administrative function and reduce costs'. You really dismiss her because she lacks initiative, is reluctant to change, is ineffective and always moaning and groaning.

You arrive late for the meeting because 'of terrible traffic jams *en route'*. You are really late because you set out late. You know there are always traffic jams on that route.

You didn't call back because 'you were exceptionally busy with an urgent problem'. The real reason: you simply didn't want to speak to that person.

You have refused the engineering supervisor training because of 'budget limitations'. Actually you just don't believe that he or she would benefit from any form of training. Hiding behind budget limitations is a typical rationalization, or blaming personnel for inaction, or the board. Others hide behind pending reorganizations or external studies by consultants as an excuse for doing nothing.

You don't tell your team about the new corporate strategy because it's 'confidential'. The real reason is that you don't think they'd understand and would waste a lot of your precious time asking stupid questions and raising petty objections.

Rationalization creates a climate of simulated cosmetic understandings, easily undermined by distorted interpretations and disbelief. Everyone joins in the game, creating a veneer of plausibility which obscures the deep understanding requisite for managerial competence and success. An escalation takes place whereby major judgements are based on this veneer of superficial understanding, where reasons are accepted without challenge, where there is total failure to differentiate between an excuse and a justification. People guess at the answers, often relying on anecdotal evidence. The guesswork and anecdotal support becomes the rationale behind the decision.

As always there is a simple solution. As always it is incredibly difficult to apply. Those leaders who really succeed create a healthy climate of challenge. Part of their cultural norm is that the team benefits when everyone can challenge each other. Part of the norm is that reasons are rarely accepted at face value, that team members including the boss welcome having their reasons challenged, for in that way they learn and the organization benefits. The process of challenge stimulates a debate about the real reasons for a prospective decision, and in that way better decisions are arrived at. The process of challenge filters out the bad reasons – such as ulterior motives – for wanting a decision. The process of challenge flushes out the honest reasons behind some recent incident or behaviour. The process of challenge, to be effective, must be based on a trust that personal dignity will not be affronted and self-esteem preserved.

Rationalization is an insidiously dangerous threat to competence, credibility, integrity and inspiration, often overwhelming a person who is so weak, so lacking in backbone, so uncertain that he or she simulates a degree of supreme confidence. Such people have a reason for everything. The danger is that the person becomes convinced that he or she knows the real reasons when the real reasons are not known.

> 'Whenever this new managing director speaks he gives the impression that everything that went on before his arrival was bad. He didn't like the bureaucracy he found, he didn't like the personnel process we had, he didn't like our attitude towards customer service, he didn't like the cumbersome organization structure. I guess he didn't like us! Yet we've worked exceptionally hard for this company and made it one of the most successful in its field. I think he's trying to make his mark with the board by trying to change things for the sake of it. Either that or he's trying to enhance his own credibility by making out his predecessor was useless, that he effectively inherited a shambles from him. I think it's a worse shambles now with him. I've got no confidence he'll succeed. He's certainly alienated most of us around here.'

Superbosses trust their people to make the best decisions in any given circumstance. Such bosses don't go round asking their people always to justify their decisions. What these bosses do is encourage people to have their prospective decisions challenged. It is not the same as asking permission. It is saying, 'Boss, I need your help in making this difficult decision. It's my decision, boss, but perhaps you can help check out the rationale behind it.'

Find the real reasons and communicate them openly and honestly, but don't invent them through rationalization.

19

Prejudice: the invidious management disease

'"All bosses are bad, all trade unions are irresponsible." Prejudice runs deep in many organizations.'

There is prejudice against the personnel function, prejudice against the so-called militant shop stewards, prejudice against bosses who drive fast BMWs. Sometimes the prejudice is more insidious – prejudice against women or ethnic minorities. Nobody admits it but the minutiae of behaviour shows it.

Prejudice is based on half-truths if not ignorance. It is the ingrained habit of making judgements without having elicited, weighed up and challenged all the available facts. It is the ingrained habit of not giving others the benefit of the doubt. It is the ingrained habit of attempting to establish one's own credibility by diminishing that of others.

Prejudice distorts judgement. Any proposal from the trade union will be 'bad', perceived as having an ulterior motive (screw the company) or a hidden agenda (the thin end of the wedge).

Conversely, whatever management does is perceived by the union as less than half of what they could do. History is scraped for anecdotes to support this. The good bits of management are ignored as the bad bits are dredged up from the distant past and converted into organization myths about exploitative bosses.

120

Trade-union leaders are branded as rabble-rousers, trouble-makers and exploiters of their members' ignorance. Few managers dare challenge the deeply held view that all shop stewards are aggressive, argumentative, unreasonable and full of emotional rhetoric. The nice shop steward is perceived as weak, as having no 'clout'. The incredibly bad bosses see the trade unions as incapable of any understanding, as only being there for one thing – irrespective of the greater good of the company – and that's for the short-term benefit of their members.

Integrity and credibility is simulated through a process of gentle-manly conduct whereby bosses and trade-union officials are the best of friends informally and then slang each other in public. Such hypocrisy is accepted as part of the game, par for the course.

The prejudice bites deep into the organization. Nothing is certain except the rhetoric of the prejudiced manager or shop steward. Facts are irrelevant. What is important is that managers are bad (if you are a trade unionist) or that trade unions are totally irresponsible (if you are a manager). Personnel people tend to see both sides and therefore invite a prejudicial view of them as being chameleons, people without principle or backbone who run with the hares and hunt with the hounds.

As prejudice surfaces power over-rides fact. The power of the rhetoric suppresses the power of the truth – at least in the short term. Truth is not a valuable commodity in traditional employee relations. Truth does not yield the best pay deals, nor the best profit levels – depending upon which side you are on.

This prejudicial power is exploited at the expense of weaker groups who need care and protection but have no one to represent their interests. Such is the prejudice against women, against ethnic minorities, against people who are disabled, against anyone outside the 'group'.

It is the power of the jungle. Prejudice is the antithesis of civiliza-tion. Every fox thinks every man is a fox-killer. Would you kill a fox? Probably not, but the fox will run from you.

Superbosses are incredibly sensitive to the dangers of prejudice within their organizations. Aware that they themselves as bosses, can be infected by prejudice as easily as a common cold, they are forever challenging their own judgements, views and opinions. They resist the temptation of jumping to conclusions as a result of isolated aspects of behaviour. They go hunting for all the facts (not just those that suit them) and analyse these carefully before coming to a conclusion.

'I'm a woman in an all-male department. I think they resent me. They don't know how to handle me because I'm articulate, intelligent I think, and dress well. I find I don't get notified of meetings, I don't get the paperwork – I accidentally get missed off distribution lists.

'They organize pre-meetings but don't tell me. First time I went to the departmental meeting nobody welcomed me, nobody introduced me. They just ignored me as I entered the room.

'I took the matter up with my boss and he just threw up his hands in laughter. "Your problem, my dear, is you take things personally," he told me. "That's the trouble with you women, you're too sensitive."'

The elimination of prejudice in management, especially in industrial relations, sexism, race and disability should be one of the highest priority goals a boss should have.

Prejudice brings out the worst in people. It can divide and destroy an organization.

20

Closed minds

'When you taste rotten food you spit it out.
When you detect an obnoxious smell you cover your
nose.
When you see an unpleasant sight you turn your
eye.
When you hear the unpalatable truth you close
your mind.'

> 'The only way of getting your message through to senior management
> is to hire a consultant at vast expense and have him tell them what
> they refuse to hear from you. It always works. They listen to con-
> sultants but never listen to us.'

In the never-ending personal pursuit of credibility, status and
standing in the eyes of others, there is a tendency to reject any
data which seeks to diminish that credibility. Bad news is all
right as long as it affects other people only. But we don't like to
be told our breath smells, or that we are long-winded and boring, or slow and ineffective, or indecisive, or lacking in moral
fibre, or subservient to our boss, or too easy on our team, or
arrogant, or untrustworthy, or negligent, or inept. The list goes
on, a list of words we frequently use about other people but
rarely about ourselves.

We close our minds to the possibility that we can be as bad as we
make others out to be.

Sometimes we denigrate ourselves in acceptable ways to invoke a crediting response from our colleagues, but in doing so we still close our mind to the real problem, wishing our colleagues to tell us there is no problem, that we are better than we think.

Self-doubt and vulnerability, uncertainty and loss of confidence become a tangle of distorted emotions from which it is difficult to extract the truth about oneself, the truth being such that it would be likely to induce more self-doubt, vulnerability, uncertainty and loss of confidence if revealed. We protect ourselves from this frightening downward spiral by developing a protective shell of projected credibility, trying to impress people with our achievements, good will and good intent. As if they didn't know, we force upon them our good points, our standing. We let them know who we know (if they are important – like the chief executive).

The impression we attempt to create is frequently divorced from the reality and frequently divorced from the perceptions others hold of us. Reality becomes obscured as we trade impressions and perceptions. The unwelcome light of negative truth jars against the sanitized but distorted images with which we comfort ourselves.

Such is the closed mind. We open our mind to praise, either false or genuine, but close it to criticism. We open our mind to good news but close it to bad, preferring to criticize the communicator's perception.

We don't want to know morale is low, so we convince ourselves it is high. One anecdotal remark in the bar is enough to convince us. When retention plummets and low morale is eventually proven we reject any suggestion that it might be due to our atrocious style of leadership, or due to our failure to communicate, involve, value people and recognize their unique contribution. So we convince ourselves that other factors predominate – like the company's laggard pay policy in relation to high-paying hijackers in the marketplace.

We will just about accept the bad news as long as there is no suggestion that it was us who caused it.

Few of us own up to the personal responsibility for a disaster or mismanagement. It's always someone else. The erosion of competence and effectiveness is always elsewhere in the organization if not due to external factors. We close our mind to the dreadful possibility that it could be us. That would hurt too much, it would destroy our self-esteem in the face of others.

We are the large majority of incredibly bad bosses, forever on the defensive, forever skirting blame, forever resisting responsibility for failure while claiming credit for success. We are the closed-minded majority who close off real opportunities for learning and real success.

The solution is simple. It is derived from two basic beliefs a credible boss will hold:

1. that he or she is as fallible as any other person within the organization;
2. that there is always an opportunity to do better tomorrow.

Superbosses discipline themselves to keep their minds forever open. They always listen and as a result are always learning. They learn never to be dismissive of other people's comments, ideas, criticism, feedback, complaints. Furthermore they encourage within their teams a process of challenge and constructive criticism – even when levelled at themselves. They never close their minds to the possibility that they could be wrong, that they could improve. Humility is of the essence to an incredibly successful boss. Arrogance, self-righteousness and a closed mind might bring short-term results but long-term success never.

> 'I've run payroll now for ten years. Never once have we missed a pay deadline. This new director came on board and we received an instruction from him that all staff had to attend a meeting Thursday afternoon. I told him it was pay-day and we had to get the payroll out, therefore my team would be unable to attend. "I don't care about that!" he told me, "I want everyone to come to this meeting." I ignored him so we could get our payroll out. He hasn't spoken to me since!'

The reality is that we are all highly imperfect and will continue to be so till the day we die. The opportunity, seized by the more creditable bosses is to eliminate some of these imperfections in a step-by-step personal improvement process.

The start point, as always, is to look at ourselves and discover the amazing opportunities the world presents us when we open our mind to discover what we really are.

21

Sycophancy

'Sycophancy is the art of ingratiation through the simulation of motivation.'

The sycophant is blind to his own self in becoming a mere extension of other people, helping them reinforce their own distorted perceptions of what they'd like to be and think they are.

Sycophants live in an unreal world of their own making, a world where the chief executive is perfect, or highly imperfect, depending on whom they are talking to.

Sycophants embody the projected values and beliefs of others while totally devoid of their own. In losing sight of themselves in favour of others they constantly change their principles and opinions according to whom they are talking.

Sycophants have little knowledge of themselves and only marginally more knowledge of their patrons.

Sycophancy brings an emulation of credibility. Without any real credibility themselves they syphon off and live upon, like leeches, the credibility and reputation of their masters and mistresses. They grab their importance from the important people they work for. Some even pretend to be the boss when the boss is not around.

Surrounded by sycophants the poor boss conjures up a distorted perception of her own great doings and of the terrible perpetrations of others.

Other than nominally, sycophants never challenge their bosses. Such bosses, autocratic as they are, do not welcome challenge and prefer to wallow in the illusory comfort which sycophancy provides.

By comparison the best bosses welcome challenge and even learn to live with the pain. Great achievements are never without pain *en route.*

Sycophants rarely disagree with their bosses. Such bosses always believe they are right and wallow in consent.

By comparison the best bosses welcome healthy and constructive disagreement. It is the way they and their people learn.

Sycophants and their bosses rarely learn. All they do is perpetuate their own ignorance in an unreal world of illusion. An illusion that they are great and the rest of the world rotten. Such is their perception of trade unions, the competition, middle managers, personnel and any other person or group who has the audacity to pretend to know better and question their authority and expertise.

Companies go out of business, top bosses fail because of sycophancy. Senior echelons of many organizations often become infested with highly paid sycophants whose sole purpose in life is to ingratiate themselves and please top people.

Progress and achievement are synonymous with challenge. Suppress challenge internally or externally and there will be no long-term success. Sycophancy is the pleasant art of suppressing challenge in favour of ingratiation. It prevails in many organizations.

Ingratiation disguises subjectivity. Subordinates give bosses what they like to hear, confirming the bosses' view that they are right, reinforcing the great image they like to hold of themselves.

To be 'in' with the bosses, to have their 'ear' becomes part of the ingratiation process. Bosses favour it, wanting to develop good relationships with others, especially those they can trust, especially those who admire them.

Together the boss and the ingratiating sycophants around her become a tribe within the organization, exhibiting a prowess which they claim to be high performance. Those outside the tribal boundary are normally deemed deficient in the required tribal qualities.

The tribe is not necessarily the boss's formal team within the organization. Dissenters who fail to ingratiate themselves with the boss are cast aside, are ejected beyond the tribal boundaries to the cold, formal hierarchical reaches of the second team. There they snipe at the boss who from time to time reaches out to feed them snippets of stale organization news through the formal communication process. These outcasts are rarely involved in the decisions made by the boss and her team of sycophants. They are rarely consulted or listened to. They have little power to influence.

Performance deterioration as a result of the ingratiation process, if recognized, is blamed on external forces. The organization is accused of failing to provide the tribal chief with the tools to deal with the outcasts, for example 'hire and fire' tools, compensation tools, transfer tools.

In this jungle the tribal chiefs only perceive 'good people' (those who ingratiate themselves with them) and 'bad people' (those who don't). Little does the tribal chief know that many who ingratiate are two-faced and ingratiate themselves with other important people, even rivals, beyond the tribal boundary. Sycophants keep their options open in case of re-organization.

> 'Since the new chief executive came in, life has become one big promotion interview. All the senior managers are going around looking smart, speaking his language and saying all the right things. They're all trying to impress. They know that half the directors will be retiring within the next two or three years. Meanwhile you try getting a decision made!'

Credible bosses see through attempts at ingratiation. They ride it without accepting it. The pleasing smile, the rush to agree with what they say they find unnerving. These bosses like to be challenged by people with conviction.

Credible bosses surround themselves with a wide circle of people who are prepared to challenge them. There is no place for sycophancy and ingratiation within this circle.

22

Management by intimidation

'It is incredible how many organizations there are around in which employees feel intimidated by their bosses. A culture of fear prevails.'

> 'It's no good speaking up. They just shout you down, put a black mark against you. You become a marked man, there's no hope then. So I just keep my head down, say nothing, do my job till 5.00 p.m. and then escape home.'

Employees are often frightened of telling the truth, as they see it, for fear of putting their organization in a bad light and their jobs and promotion prospects at risk.

Bosses develop insidious techniques for intimidating their people. Voluminous rule books are devised to keep people in line with the bosses' thinking. 'Thou shalt not spend a penny without my permission' becomes a dominant ethos. People who step out of line are cast out as lepers, to be mistrusted, never to be promoted, let alone listened to.

'He who takes an initiative is attacking the boss, for not having taken that initiative before. He is accusing me of having got it wrong.'

'She who speaks her mind is getting at the boss. How dare she disagree!'

'We the bosses know best!' is their constant assertion and anyone thinking otherwise should be fearful of the consequences.

When the strike comes poor innocent employees are torn between two opposing intimidatory forces. The union leaders threaten every sort of sanction, including violence against those who do not support the union. And the organization bosses threaten every sort of sanction, including loss of job, against those who do not support the organization.

Yet fear is a destructive force. From those who study animals to those who plunge their companies into bankruptcy it has been proven that fear is the worst type of motivating force. While it can yield high performance in the short term, long term it erodes the whole moral fibre of the organization and subsequently induces rebellion. Performance rots away as people learn to cope with their fear by developing defence mechanisms against those who intimidate them.

> **The previous board was paranoid, intimidating. It was a frightening and depressing experience to attend it. Now with the new chief executive there is a breath of fresh air. The board works as if it were a team. There is a general sense that they are trying to achieve things, and that's beginning to filter down through the organization.'**

The most common fear in modern organizations is that of 'speaking up'. Bad bosses cover up their intimidatory instincts with simulated communications. But those who speak up get slapped down with dismissive accusations of 'not understanding', of 'being negative'. They are branded as troublemakers, of being dissidents within the organization. At best those who speak up are fobbed off with stock answers that convince no one and serve only to delude the senior managers who mouth them.

Intimidation precludes the opportunity to discover the truth, to assess the reality of what's happening in the organization. Those intimidated concoct answers to appease their oppressors who in turn are readily convinced they are doing great jobs as leaders.

Anyone who has a contrary opinion has obviously got it wrong, doesn't understand.

Accusations of disloyalty and other forms of emotional black-mail are used to intimidate employees from speaking their mind. 'The new product might be unreliable' but if you advise the customers of that you are being disloyal. 'We don't want disloyal people in this organization.'

The very best leaders realize that fear is a vital force in motivation and performance. But it is a natural force which need never be exploited through intimidatory management. Fear must come from within, the fear of failure, the fear of letting others down, the fear of being dishonest, the fear of doing a bad job. The fear of atrocious service to the customer, of faulty workmanship, of unsafe practices. In the end fear will act upon the conscience. Such fear is natural and should never be dispelled in the pursuit of excellence. Who fears complacency?

To develop a highly motivated team capable of incredible levels of performance the superboss develops a set of shared values and beliefs which all the team is fearful of deviating from.

The worst leaders intimidate because they uphold and impose values and beliefs to which their team do not subscribe nor possibly understand.

If punctuality, high quality and superb customer service are shared values then every team member will be fearful of failing

---

'It's all right the top bosses talking about "delegation and devolve-ment" in introducing this new style of management, but I can't get my people to accept responsibility. They haven't been trained nor will these new bosses allow me any budget to train them. My people are frightened of making decisions. There's enough recent evidence in their minds that if you make a bad decision you get a kick up the backside. And the next time you get fired. They all think, and I do too, that this new regime is fostering a "hire and fire" culture. People are frightened. The best thing you can do is keep your head down.'

to accomplish them. There will be no intimidation. At worst people let themselves down.

If strict cost control, adherence to rule books and deference to the boss and values are beliefs upheld only by the boss and imposed by him or her, then every team member will be fearful of the boss. Intimidation will occur. At worst people let the boss down.

When you let other people down you should fear yourself, not them.

23

Rituals

'All organizations have their rituals.'

- The chairman's ritual walkabout at Christmas. It is not clear what it achieves.
- The ritual complaint by the trade union about the company's derisory pay offer.
- The ritual training of certain groups to ease their bosses' consciences and appease aspirations.
- The ritual completion of performance appraisal as a gesture towards progressive management.
- The ritual clocking in.

Rituals are automatic behaviours evolved over a period of time, behaviours which few challenge, behaviours which often serve no better purpose than to present a façade of good management.

Initially there may have been a genuine reason for the behaviour. But the behaviour becomes repeated without too much further thought. It develops into a ritual. People do it because they've always done it.

Rituals are difficult to challenge as there is always a semblance of reason behind them. Clocking in has its reason, the chairman's Christmas walkabout has its reason. But today those could be bad reasons. Managers don't clock in – why should others? The chairman does not walk around at other times of the year.

The danger is that bosses and their people get into automatic modes of behaviour which often deflect from current organization goals and serve only to diminish the credibility and integrity of bosses who permit such rituals to go unchecked.

Rituals are difficult to eliminate because a large number of people find comfort in them. By automatic simulation of management practice they can avoid the real issues. The walkabout becomes a simulation of communication but effectively avoids the painful process of real two-way communication. Ritualistic behaviour enables people to proceed without thinking, without having to address the real problem. Rituals are the railway lines of management which take them into sidings.

'Our director is a do-gooding lost-cause person who's always getting in the way with his misunderstandings. For example he likes to make one branch visit every week. He invites all the moans and groans from the staff and they play up to him, pushing forward all their hardy perennial complaints. He comes back to head office and then sprays out memos telling us to fix these problems – as if we weren't doing our job. What he doesn't understand is that we've been trying to sort them out for years but he's never given us the budget to do so. He just doesn't understand.'

In vibrant organizations led by successful bosses you will find little ritual. Every action, every behaviour has real meaning, has real direction, is aimed at really achieving something.

In more conservative organizations the maintenance of rituals is akin to a process of fossilization. There is little dynamic of change because 'we are doing it already'. 'We do communicate, we do monitor performance, we do involve our staff.' But what they don't realize is they do it in a ritualistic way. And that way is an unthinking way. In business anybody who does something in an unthinking way must be inferior to anyone doing it in a thinking way.

Rituals are a comfortable option for the unthinking leader.

24

Totem poles

'Most of us are unaware of the rites we perform around the organization totem pole.'

Believing that we're civilized, we might frown upon the ancient totem poles of the North American Indians and their ritualistic tribal dances.

Some claim that the monarchy is the totem pole of the British nation. Because we don't think of the British throne as such there is a tendency immediately to reject the idea.

But the idea bears examination because in fact many organizations and groups of people do unwittingly develop their own totem poles and ritualistic dances around them.

In my view totem poles have their place. It is the lack of awareness of them or indeed the rejection of the very idea that is a key threat to integrity and the credibility of the organization.

A totem pole is a symbolic focus for the ritualistic and unthinking behaviours of people within the group. It symbolizes certain group values and beliefs as well as fantasies and aspirations. It provides a clear focus for a communication that often proves difficult through the conventional means of rational explanation.

'Profit' is the most traditional totem pole, representing as it does the unseen god worshipped by most industrialists. In traditional commercial organizations everyone dances to the tune of profit, celebrating its excesses and bewailing its loss. As a totem pole it symbolizes and embraces the core value and *raison d'être* of what business is supposed to be about.

With advances in corporate thinking many business leaders saw the limitation of the crude profit totem. So the progressive companies of the 1980s began to develop more sophisticated totem poles around which their people could dance, for example: 'productivity', 'quality', 'excellence' and 'customer care'.

My totem poles are competence, credibility and integrity. To me they symbolize what all successful organizations should be about. Without any one of them there can never be long-term success. With all of them long-term success can be sustained.

> 'My boss only thinks money, to him it's everything. He's got no appreciation of what people mean to the organization. You start talking people language to him and his eyes glaze over, he doesn't understand people issues.'

Totem poles provide an abstract focus for what I believe are the core values and beliefs necessary for this 'dreamed of' success in the organization. They are totem poles because the concepts extend beyond sheer rationality, embracing as they do the spirit, emotions, aspirations and fantasies of an organization and its people.

In a sophisticated world one doesn't need to dance around carved wooden poles. A word is sufficient. That word might be profit. What is yours?.

25

Taboos

'Taboos should be identified, challenged and eliminated.'

Inarticulated taboos evolve within most organizations.

It would be taboo to criticize the company's advertising in front of the marketing director. It would be taboo to suggest to the board that they have been consistently weak by caving in to the trade union.

It would be taboo to indicate to the chief executive that her recent re-organization was a complete bungle, totally unnecessary and has alienated a lot of good people. It would be taboo to say to a union representative that you are against trade unions, as you are. It would be taboo to challenge the board about their privi-

---

'The trade has this major exhibition once a year. Only the senior executives in our company are allowed to go. When I was a junior I asked whether I could attend. My boss came back and said, "No!" A week before the exhibition one of my major accounts rang through and said he had a couple of tickets and would like me to attend the exhibition with him. I tried to get hold of my boss but he was away on a trip. So I decided to go, thinking it important to please the customer.

'On the day of the exhibition I approached our company's stand to show it to the dealer who'd brought me along. Standing there on the platform, hands behind his back was one of our directors. He saw me approaching. "What the hell are you doing here!" he yelled at me in front of the dealer, "You've got no right to attend this exhibition!" The dealer was aghast, we lost the account. Two months later the same dealer hired me as a senior account executive.'

---

leged dining facilities, their Concorde trips or expensive hospitality tents at Henley.

It would be taboo to enquire about your boss's salary, or why 'so and so' was fired, or why the slender blonde from accounts got the job which everyone thought one of her more senior colleagues would get.

It would be taboo to ask the production manager to confirm the rumours that he is having an affair with his secretary.

Taboos are 'no-go' areas, created informally within an organization to protect people from unwelcome challenge.

Ideally when total integrity is achieved within an organization few taboos will be left, perhaps only those pertaining to personal intimacy. The elimination of taboos creates a more open and honest organization where people feel free to express their feelings, resolve ambiguities and challenge decisions they don't understand.

As a boss don't deceive yourself that there are no taboos surrounding you. Confront them. You might be surprised at what you find.

26

The denigration syndrome

'Attempting to enhance your own credibility by diminishing that of others is the classic symptom of the "denigration syndrome".'

> 'On the hundredth time my boss ran me down in front of the team I decided I'd had enough. I resigned. He swore at me when I did, saying he'd give me a lousy reference. I still haven't found another job.'

In the pursuit of illusory success it takes little to denigrate other departments by exposing their people's weaknesses in comparison to your alleged strengths.

It is always the others who are falling behind, not pulling their weight, not being straight, not keeping to the rules, not conforming to the high standards you allege you maintain.

Pay problems are personnel's fault. You denigrate personnel. Late deliveries are the fault of sales administration. You put them down too. Lack of authority to purchase a simple piece of equipment is the fault of the board. You are always belittling them. And so it goes on. It is always someone else's fault. You do them 'down' and thereby establish your own credibility as a winner. But it is an illusion.

You deceive yourself. You erode your own integrity. By building up your own department and yourself as the best and establishing others as the worst you create divisiveness, élitism, arrogance, lack of co–operation. Everyone's credibility is eroded as perceptions of competence become grossly distorted.

The denigration syndrome can result in gross alienation all around you.

> 'Our boss hates us taking days off. Last month I went and asked him for one day off. It was my daughter's graduation ceremony. He really humiliated me, made out I was being disloyal, letting the side down, had no sense of responsibility when we had all this urgent work on.
>
> 'So I went sick for the day. "Stuff him," I thought.'

Credible bosses denigrate nobody. Pay problems are their problem, not personnel's. Late deliveries are their problem, not sales administration's. Lack of authority is their problem, not the board's.

Those sad managers who are forever making disparaging remarks fall into the trap of projecting their problems on to others. They can't even see that it's their problem.

It's obvious to them that their lack of success is due to other factors, for example interest rates, exchange problems, trade unions, government policy and so on. There's nothing they can do about it – except blame others in a debilitating process of denigration.

Politics is rife with denigration. No matter the merit of the other side's case nor the capability of the person presenting it, that case and the person will be put down. It is the same with internal politics within organizations.

Credible bosses don't blame external factors either. They accept the constraints and find a way through despite them.

> 'Every time we raise an issue with him at our team meeting he slaps us down. He becomes totally dismissive, accusing us of not understanding, of being unreasonable, of being negative. So we don't raise issues with him any longer. We just sit there and pretend to listen. It's a real bore!'

The denigration syndrome can spread rapidly through an organization. Ultimately everyone pulls down the organization.

Concentrate on resolving your own problems but don't denigrate other people because of theirs.

27

Inner circles, clans and clubs

'Trust is a commodity in short supply. One begins life by trusting everyone, lives life with that trust gradually being eroded and ends life with that trust confined to a small inner circle of family, friends and acquaintances.'

While successful leaders go out of their way to develop the trust essential for a high performing and motivated team, less successful bosses progressively restrict their trust to an inner circle of colleagues who share the same moans and groans.

It is these inner circles and clans within organizations which effectively divide and create dissent. They weaken the spirit of organizations and thereby restrict success if not contribute to failure. Such inner circles attempt to broke power, conspiring to establish clandestine networks of influence, withholding vital information from those outside the circle who need it, while sprinkling the grapevine with distorted half-truths. They are forever lobbying on behalf of the group while insidiously denigrating others outside the group.

These inner circles and clans evolve over a period of time and inevitably are at variance with the formal hierarchical structures within the organization. Their goals vary too in that their dissent is induced by a perceived failure of the organization to meet their needs.

Such cliques and clubs merely serve to undermine the integrity of the organization, perhaps because the organization was lacking in integrity in the first place. Similarly the credibility of specific executives is undermined or reinforced according to their association with or potential support of the group. Loyalties are split accordingly.

The clan might well, for example, gang up against an unwelcome new member assigned to the team by the hierarchy. The clan will contrive to limit co-operation with this person, desisting from social interaction and creating a cold, alien climate in order to isolate the foreigner and encourage a quick departure from the group.

Outside the inner circle no one is trusted. To be accepted within the circle you have to demonstrate allegiance and complete trust. You have to 'speak the right language' – more often a language of contrived dissent. You have to conform to the norms and values of the group, norms and values which would not be endorsed by senior management.

Inner circles, clans and cliques are like destructive micro-organisms drifting around an organization, scavenging for support for their alien causes, excreting poisons to undermine the moral fibre of rival teams and their bosses.

People feel comfortable and secure in these inner circles. They seek refuge in them from the rigours of an oppressively hostile organization. Within these cliques people find soulmates and others of like mind. They seek to develop their own informal credibility at a time when the organization dispenses them little. They have their own code of integrity at a time they perceive their senior bosses having none. Members of the inner circle reinforce each other's credibility while doing everything to diminish the credibility of those outside.

To prevent the potentially damaging effect of inner circles super-bosses work to create a climate of trust throughout their organisations whether large or small. They seek to include every single employee within the circle, to make every individual a member of the club. They work hard to avoid having anyone excluded from communications, from involvement in decision-making processes, from participation in key activities. They seek to create an organization where everyone shares the same values, beliefs and subscribes to the accomplishment of the corporate vision. They have sensitive antennae which tune in to any signals that certain individuals or groups (cliques) are beginning to go their own way with their own divergent philosophy and vision.

> 'I got no induction when I joined this department, not even a welcome. I just turned up and sat at a desk where there were some papers marked for my attention. Nobody told me where the toilets were, how to get coffee, where to go for lunch, who to sit with. I had to find out for myself. Nobody introduced me to the other people on the floor, I had to go round asking. I didn't see my boss the first morning. He turned up in the afternoon. "You all right?" he asked as he passed my desk. Before I could answer he'd moved on!'

Organization integrity means a total integration of beliefs, values, customs and words within the group. It doesn't mean programming people to behave consistently in accordance with the policy manual; in fact, with the high value placed on trust, people have many delegated freedoms to contribute to the achievement of the vision, freedoms to innovate and invent new more effective methods, freedoms to challenge a system which forever will need developing, freedom to express their views.

Inner circles and cliques are best avoided when the boss creates an organization in which people can openly and honestly criticize the organization itself, and furthermore know that the bosses will take careful account of these criticisms.

Creating a wide, open circle of believers and organization challengers is the best route to competence and success.

28

Managerial helplessness

'It is incredible how many middle managers in large organizations feel helpless.'

> 'In this company there is only one policy: "More for less". They are always expecting us to do extra, new projects, new systems, reports on this, investigations into that. But we never ever get any additional resource no matter how much we ask. It's going to end up by most of us not doing the jobs we're being paid to do.'

In the long distant past they have attempted to take on their company and its large corporate bureaucracy but have failed, their attempts to change things have always been frustrated by the 'system' or so they say.

Such managers become cynical, defeatist, despairing. They blame the company for their inability to change anything. Furthermore they become sceptical of any change initiatives from centralized departments or new bosses. They see the company conspiring against them in their quest to do better for it.

They say they need more staff but have to go through tortuous nightmares to convince those above to approve the filling of even a single vacancy. They say they need to pay staff more to recruit the right type but are confronted with the standard rhetoric 'keep costs down – don't create precedents' when making the case. They say they need more hi-tech systems but come across unhelpful overburdened centralized IT departments who are unable to cope with the demand for their services. They say they need to train their staff but find the centralized training function hopelessly underfunded.

It seems that whichever way they want to turn they meet organization obstacles. 'You can't do that' appears to be the prevailing ethos. The managers don't feel trusted, don't feel valued. They feel they are mere pawns in an oppressive organization, mere instruments of the irrational whims of senior executives. At times they feel they are no more than corporate messengers.

Managerial helplessness is endemic in many large organizations.

Yet somehow, rising above this gloom, despondency, defeatism and atmosphere of repression are a minority of incredibly successful managers who seem able to cast aside these bureaucratic constraints and actually get things done. They seem able to take on the organization and succeed in obtaining and using freedoms and approaches denied others.

They become the rising stars who get promoted, who get known – and who inevitably alienate those moaners and groaners who never succeed.

How do they do it? How do they actually take on a large corporate bureaucracy which appears to contrive to constrain them?

The answer is belief. It is the conviction and courage they have within themselves. They believe in themselves. They have a clear vision of what has to be achieved and if the company appears to constrain them they have the courage to take the company on. They know how to make their case, they know how to fight their corner and they have the courage to put their jobs on the line if necessary.

These managers earn credibility. They do not use half-baked arguments, nor indulge in second-guessing. They don't back off when shouted at or shouted down. They don't give up first time round nor submit to the first skirmishing disapproval. They persist because they believe totally in the intrinsic merit of their case.

> 'I've got a great team, I love them all. But I have to protect them from these maniacs above. It's killing me. Just look at me! I'm permanently knackered. I work 14 hours a day. I work weekends. I soak up all the pressures, I take all the crap that comes down from on high so that my team can get on and do the real work. I'd retire tomorrow if it wasn't for my team. My wife thinks I'm mad. "You're killing yourself for this company," she tells me, "and they don't give a damn for you."'

Managerial helplessness is endemic because most managers don't know how to help themselves. They have been trained to expect help from elsewhere – and then get disappointed when it doesn't arrive on a plate.

Managerial helplessness exists only when managers expect too much from the organization and too little from themselves.

Part 4

INTEGRITY GAPS

The incredible behaviour of many bosses leads to huge integrity gaps (reflected as credibility gaps) to be found in many organizations.

●

In this part of the book some of these gaps are explored. Inevitably the greater the number of gaps and the larger they are, the higher the risk of failure.

1

Erosion of integrity

'Without thinking we erode integrity.'

> 'We have a manipulative culture in this organization. The bosses manipulate you to get what they want, smiling one day, mouthing platitudes the next, and making threats the day after. We understand the game, it doesn't take us in. In return we manipulate them to get what we want – otherwise no one would bother about us. For example if you have equipment which breaks down it's impossible to get it repaired – they're short of engineering staff at the workshop, it's also impossible to get new equipment because of budgetary constraints. So we beg, borrow and steal equipment from other departments. In that way we don't let our clients down. It's the same with working hours: they expect you to work 14 hours a day 6 days a week because we're so short-staffed. They never give you time off in lieu nor do they have an overtime budget. So we just go sick when we need a rest. It's all a game. Nobody bothers.'

Loss of customer confidence, low staff morale and poor performance result from the erosion of integrity within an organization. A customer who fails to get service might well have encountered a disinterested employee who is led by a boss too busy to bother about the attitudes of his people.

Corporate gloss, rendered like paintwork across company reports, brochures and advertisements, has little value if inconsistent with the day-by-day practices within an organization. In a long, frustrating queue a 'customer-first charter' becomes worthless. Making yourself out to be what you are not is an erosion of integrity.

153

For example, here is an extract from the mission statement of one large organization: *'Our most important assets are our people. Their motivation, development, well being and effective deployment are fundamental to our future success.'* In my first few encounters with this organization I did not meet one manager or employee who believed this statement. No one was aware of any specific action to implement these pious words written by the chief executive. Most saw the statement as mere words on paper which at best the board paid lip-service to.

> 'The new company slogan is "We do it better." Like hell we do! We pay our staff less, we talk about training but rarely do it, our office conditions are appalling – for example the furniture we have is 20 years old and falling to bits. Our retention is lousy and the personnel function is hopeless – no help at all. As far as I'm concerned the slogan is totally meaningless.'

If people are an organization's most important asset, where was the evidence in practice? All I encountered was low morale and dissatisfaction. Training was neglected and there was low pay, poor retention rates and not surprisingly an erosion of customer confidence. The example is common.

> 'I used to come to work happy, really looking forward to it. It's different now since the re-organization. Every time I enter the building it's like being submerged in a giant black cloud. My morale is sapped, I can't see where the organization is going. There are phenomenal short-term pressures now and nobody is really prepared to help, it's everyone for themselves.
>
> 'I can't get to see my boss, he's always too busy, yet I get reams of memos from him. He's part of the black cloud.
>
> 'No longer can I come to work and get on with my work – or what I think it is. I seem to spend all my time on paperwork, on committees, on short-term expedient action.
>
> 'Everyone's looking over their shoulders now. There's no stability now and really no opportunity to go forward and provide a better service to our customers. In fact it's worse now.'

Many managers mouth appeasements which, while sounding good, they make little attempt to implement. Such is the erosion of integrity.

All but the best managers are full of such contradictions, contradictions which erode the integrity of the less capable manager.

To prevent the erosion of integrity the best bosses ensure that their words are consistent with their actions.

2

Hypocrisy

'Making out to be what you are not is the mark of a hypocrite. Such managers do not know themselves.'

'They are just a load of charlatans. They (the bosses) make promises they never keep. At the team meeting I raised the question of our third-party business and how we're getting squeezed on margins all the while. My recommendation was we should pull out of this type of business altogether. My boss and the director, who was present, promised they would consider the suggestion and report back. That was a year ago. They never reported back. I've raised it twice since then. They just waffle on, oozing platitudes and bland statements. But we never get a direct answer.'

If you don't know who you are you will be driven by events. If you are driven by events you will say one thing one moment and do the opposite the next. You will lose credibility and become branded as a hypocrite.

You will say you believe in employee development and two months later slash the training budget. You will say you believe in good communications but never have time enough to get your team together. You will say you believe in fair pay and then screw your people down on wage costs. You will encourage people to bring their problems to you and then make them feel bad when they do so. You will tell your deputy that she is doing well and the next minute tell your boss you have reservations about her. You will convince your customers it's an excellent product while being very worried about the quality of the design.

You will pretend to enjoy social evenings with the trade-union representatives while hating every minute. You will tell your employees you value their dedication, loyalty, commitment and hard work while being concerned for the state of their morale, the increasing absenteeism and threatened strikes. You will say to the prospective supplier that you will contact him in due course while never intending to do so. You will say you will phone back knowing you won't. You will say 'That's a good idea' and then do nothing about it.

You will tell your boss that you can't attend the committee because of an urgent meeting with a customer, when the real reason lies elsewhere. You will declare an intention to look into the regrading issue and then forget all about it. You will promise to debrief your team after every board meeting and then cancel six debriefing sessions in a row because of pressing problems. You will say you believe in performance appraisal but never find time to do one. You will say you believe in being honest with people and then ingratiate yourself with those in power while stabbing others in the back.

'The chief executive comes down regularly and does his "walking the patch" bit because the text-books say so and because he went on this training course last year. It's all bit of a farce really. He gives us a little pep talk and then invites questions. "I really want you to open up," he tells us. We know him better. At the session in June I raised the issue of company cars. He slapped me down immediately. "This isn't a negotiating forum," he said angrily. "Let's talk about something positive. We have too much negativeness at middle-management level in this organization. Let's get away from the belly-aches and complaints and concentrate on some important issues."

'He asks us to open up and is then totally dismissive when we do. So now we ask innocuous questions and he's quite happy.

'He will never learn. I just don't know how he got there.'

Most organizations are full of them. You are one of them if any of the above applies to you. You are a hypocrite. You have little credibility, little integrity. You are incredible!

Close the gap today and avoid being a hypocrite. Get into the habit of doing exactly what you say you will do.

3

Deceiving the public

'Deceiving the public has now become a professional activity.'

The process of integrity erosion within an organization will inevitably lead to large numbers of managers and employees subscribing to the rejection of certain fundamental values. Lying to the public becomes an acceptable (but semi-corrupt) value. Public affairs departments are created to 'cover up' unpalatable truths and present their organizations in the best light. Statistics are carefully selected to support the organization's case, very damaging data being filtered out. The value of objectivity is rejected and supplanted by a form of subjective representation akin to the worst type of exhortative propaganda.

Today I read that a senior staff member of a large drug company faked evidence which appeared to refute links between birth pills and heart disease. Yesterday I read that the government suppressed a report that linked poor health to levels of income.

At a mundane everyday level there are thousands of instances where organizations attempt to deceive the public with biased and distorted stories about how good they are and how allegations of shortcomings are totally wrong. Last week I read of a local fast-food restaurant denying any accountability for a piece of glass found by a customer in one of their pies. Apparently the fast-food chain blames the company who supplied the fruit filling. The supplier also denies it. Someone's lying about their accountability for the quality of the food in the restaurant.

The erosion of integrity has been institutionalized into a whole profession, that of public relations or public affairs supported by a sophisticated legal machine. Irrespective of the facts or the merit of the case the aim is always to win the hearts and minds of the public, to get people on your side. Just look at the strike leaders appearing on television. Then look at the employers. Who do you believe? It would not be surprising if you said 'Neither!'

It is not 'the done thing' to tell the truth to the public when things go wrong. Any employee who does so is at risk of being dismissed. Democracy and free speech are fine for ordinary people in the outside world but are absolutely forbidden in many large organizations. Corporate admission of failure becomes a cardinal sin. It takes a heavyweight and independent judicial investigation to expose such sin. Few people stand up and say, 'The disaster was my fault.'

The deception of the public through the erosion of integrity is only at the surface of a semi-corrupt organization wherein every employee is encouraged to suppress and hide imperfections. Such deceptions are incredibly dangerous.

Regrettably public deception has become the accepted corporate norm.

'We had a real big quality problem on Line 3. We were instructed to ship the goods out. We all knew they were defective. They should have been scrapped but we were told to do as we were told, the decision had been made at the highest level. God knows what would have happened if a customer had complained or it had hit the press. We could have had a calamity on our hands.'

In the next three chapters we will look at how this deceit extends to:

1. image manipulation;
2. advertising deceptions;
3. erosion of media integrity.

4

Image manipulation

'Integrity is achieved when the image equals the reality.'

The image never quite conforms to the reality. The greater the distance between the two the greater the credibility gap, the greater the erosion of integrity. All is not as it is made out to be. The fantasy holiday becomes a nightmare of rat-infested hotels, littered beaches and polluted seas never mentioned in the brochure. The dreamlike vision of air travel masqueraded through exotic and erotic advertising images is transformed into the hell of crowded airports, check-in ordeals and countless hours of delay until take-off. The 'world's favourite airlines' do not publish their punctuality figures nor their compliments-to-complaints ratio. Paradise, whether in the Caribbean or elsewhere, only exists in the images projected by the PR professionals. The reality is often squalid by comparison.

It takes a new recruit to discover that the company which projects an 'all-caring' image doesn't seem to care. The 'great communicator' doesn't communicate and the company that says it puts its 'customer first' frequently neglects to do so.

Business fashion is to manage the image, to sell it. The reality is in danger of neglect. The customer buys the image and discovers the reality. It can be a fraudulent conversion.

New employees join the company on the basis of an 'image' projected in the impressionistic recruitment gloss only to be disillusioned by a reality which erodes the image. The words in the brochure about 'people coming first' suddenly become meaningless as employees encounter disinterested bosses and low morale. Despite the 'excellent career prospects' in the blurb the promotion prospects appear extremely limited.

It is natural to present oneself and one's products in the best light. We would all clean the paintwork (or even repaint) before the Queen came. But the Queen is part of the image, divorced from reality. The reality is the paintwork only gets cleaned when the Queen comes. Token gestures are passed off for real and projected into favourable images which delude only those who don't know. Such is the erosion of integrity. Credibility suffers. An image is projected, a token gesture made and we are then asked to believe it is for real.

Extract from an article about Ms B. Chief Executive of Advertising Agency 'A':

This is the philosophy of Agency "A". It is a good one. The idea boiled down to its basic minimum, is that the point of advertising is to pretend that things are different when, in reality, they are not. One of "A"'s clients, for instance, is "XY" whisky. There is nothing special about "XY" whisky. It is almost exactly the same as competitive brands. "The planner and the account handler", says Ms B, "had decided that we needed to take a generic whisky-drinking benefit and accrue it to ourselves, because there's no USP – Unique Selling Point – for one whisky brand over another." Or, as the agency brochure puts it, "Our task was to create a conspicuous brand difference, so that it stood out from other campaigns." Or, as Ms B herself puts it: "Whisky is whisky is whisky."

'"So," says Ms B, "the only difference is the ad. You find something that is different about the product, however small – with 'XY' it is the shape of the bottle, the name 'XY', which is the name you'd use when you were being friendly. ... We worked out that 'XY' was sociable rather than snobby. You wouldn't bring it out on special occasions. But you bring it out when your best mate comes round. So we've tried to suggest that this brand enhances male companionship situations. Or male bonding, as we call it. We've touched real human motivation, real human behaviour, and the closer you get to touch that nerve, that cord, the better the ad."'

The solution is not to reduce the image to an accurate description of the reality but to develop the reality to meet the image.

5

Advertising deceptions

'Don't be deceived! There is no place for deception in advertising. Not even self-deception.'

For some the facts don't seem to be too helpful when promoting the product. There are advertisers who betray their integrity and inject into advertisements junk words with no relation to reality. The 'privilege' offer bears no privilege. The 'exclusive' mail-shot is by no means exclusive. The 'prestige' product has no prestige. Who is deceived? Well, it's not the customer.

Today's papers carry adverts for the car 'everybody's talking about'. Are they? There are 'fantastic' offers for kitchens of which 'dreams are made of ...'. Not my dreams nor my fantasies. A well-known coffee is advertised as 'a rare experience in taste'. It's not that rare. An after-shave has 'the power to provoke'. Who, what and why?

Meaningless advertising is commonplace. It might create awareness through the synthesis of fine words but risks deception and disappointment at the same time.

The art surely is to distil the essence of a product's fine points into a meaningful image which underlines its values and excites our attention.

The problem for some is that in an overcrowded marketplace there is little to differentiate certain products from others. So images are concocted. One lager becomes 'macho' while another becomes 'yuppy'. Both lagers taste almost the same. Only the images are different. The advertisers become dream peddlers.

Sexual connotation is prevalent for the same reason. Products are projected through sexual disguises with near-naked women pretending to sell everything but the product itself. In the end people don't buy dreams. There is no product or service in the respectable world which brings sexual satisfaction.

'For some time I had contemplated leading a management buyout of our company, although, to be honest, I knew little about it.

'One day I saw this advertisement:

MANAGEMENT BUYOUTS
TAKE A LEAF OUT OF OUR BOOK

'The advertisement, for a division of a bank, promised you a book which would explain all about management buyouts.

'At the end of the advertisement it said: "For your copy, call Hilary Bates, 071–XXX YYYY" so I rang the number.

'"Can I speak to Hilary Bates?" I asked the telephonist.

'"Who?" asked the telephonist.

'"Hilary Bates!" I repeated.

'"I don't think we have anyone here by that name, let me check …"

'"I'm responding to your bank's advertisement for a book about management buyouts," I explained.

'"Oh that!" exclaimed the telephonist. "If you give me your name and address I'll make sure the brochure is posted to you today."'

It is a corruption of integrity to associate your product with fantasies which the product cannot fulfil.

6

Erosion of media integrity

'Integrity depends not only on facts but the way they are presented and why.'

Manipulation of facts to create distorted images has become the mainstay of certain media-barons. The base instincts in most of us relish such distortion. It is fascinating to hear of the VIP seen entering a massage parlour. It is intriguing to read the intimate revelations of the lady who massaged him. Such are the refractions from the glass houses we all walk in. Today's headline story in one tabloid was of the judge who keeps a young mistress. But who is the judge?

In the pursuit of integrity facts are insufficient. Equally important is the way the facts are presented. The quest for integrity behoves us to examine carefully the underlying motivation of 'the way' we do things as well as why we do them. If the 'way' we present a fact is to incite disapproval as opposed, say, to compassion, then we are in the same danger of manipulation as that of which we criticize the media.

Many of the tabloids indulge in this blatant public deception, setting themselves up on the moral high ground to pander to the public's voyeurish affinity for the less salubrious, immoral low-life.

Most of us tend to make premature judgements in the absence of available facts. As such we set ourselves up as God in the judgement of others. The media often fails, as many top bosses do, by making ill-considered value judgements which have no relevance to the public interest (or interests of the organization). It is only of interest to expose the shortcomings of an individual if they are *clearly* of detriment to the achievement of organization goals. All other shortcomings should remain within the realms of privacy and confidentiality.

There is a part of the media which abuses its power and influence through the pretence of judging what is in the public interest. It frequently achieves the opposite. Chief executives frequently do the same in judging what is in the interests of their employees (who are they to say?).

Those who have the highest integrity tend to be humble, aware that the imperfections and wrongdoings of others are equalled by their own deficiencies. The wise person makes no judgement when he sees a VIP, employee or boss entering a massage parlour. Wise employees make no judgement when they learn through the media that their chief executive is having an affair with a woman half his age. Wise people only make judgements on issues relating to their own accountabilities.

But beware, all organizations have their media!

Whether it be in advertising, projecting an image, public relations or use of the media, many organizations today deliberately set out to mislead if not deceive the public.

Is your organization one of these and if so what are you going to do about this to sustain integrity?

7

Customer insensitivity

'It all shows up at the customer interface. When there is little credibility or integrity within the organization it is the customer who suffers.'

Countless are the anecdotes of insensitivity towards the customer. Here are two only:

1. A lady's husband dies. He had life insurance. She claims. A computerized response from the insurance company asks for her husband's signature on the claim form. She writes back explaining and in return receives a cold abrupt letter from some middle manager who says she had not read the instructions properly, nor completed the claim form correctly. She writes another letter, this time of complaint to the managing director of the company. Six weeks later she receives a stereotyped letter from customer relations acknowledging her complaint. But nothing is done. Her claim is not met. She takes up the issue with a journalist on a national newspaper. He investigates. The claim is promptly paid together with a grovelling apologetic letter from the managing director.

2. A married old-age pensioner couple order an orthopaedic bed in a sale. The wife has just recovered from a hip replacement operation. The sale price is 25 per cent off the normal price. They are assured it is a genuine sale reduction and that the bed will be delivered within six weeks. After seven weeks there is no bed and no news. They ring up.

   'Another two weeks,' they are told. Nothing happens in two weeks. After a further four weeks they ring again and get bounced from one department to another, from one person to another. Nobody seems to know much about anything. Eventually after a prolonged telephone call they are told there is an indefinite delay on the delivery of the bed.

   They visit the department store to discuss the problem with view to perhaps substituting the order for a bed that might be available. There is no salesperson available in the bedding department. While waiting for one

167

they are amazed to find the self-same bed they had ordered on display at a manufacturer's clearance price of 40 per cent off the normal price. Eventually they find a salesman who gets very angry at the suggestion that the store has misled them. They cancel the order and purchase a bed elsewhere.

'Nobody really seemed to bother about us,' they remarked later.

Everyone has their pet story relating to such appalling customer service and insensitivity.

Customer insensitivity results not from one person getting it wrong but from a whole organization and thereby its leaders getting it wrong. When huge credibility gaps arise between managers and employees, between one department and another – such as sales and manufacture, they tear an organization apart with the resultant negative impact on the customer. Sales don't believe manufacturing's projected delivery dates, the warehouse supervisor doesn't believe the production manager and on it goes. Nobody trusts each other. The sales people don't bother to tell the customer because nobody bothers to tell them, and why should they bother about the customer when nobody bothers about them? Excuses are as endemic as the alleged firefighting. Everyone is chasing their tails, overheating in a total state of ineffectiveness. Nobody has time for anyone else, let alone customers.

The reality of customer-service chaos, as epitomized in the two examples above, is far removed from the pious words of 'customer-service excellence' that ooze from many companies nowadays. The reality of individual behaviour within the organization is often totally inconsistent with the customer-service mission. A yawning credibility gap appears whichever direction you look. The problem is exacerbated by creaking archaic systems, long outmoded, which nobody is motivated to challenge or change, finding it easier to blame others for consequential inefficiency. Sales blames manufacturing, manufacturing blames administration, administration blames management services, management services blames personnel, personnel blames senior management who in turn blame their employees. And on it goes.

In such chaos customer complaints proliferate to such an extent that a 'system' is set up to handle them, thereby by-passing the very leaders who should be accountable for agonizing over them. Managing directors and senior executives are always too busy on 'more important things' to bother replying to individual complaints. So they delegate to Customer Relations who delegate to the word processor. The word processor has no heart and doesn't know the husband has died nor what an ordeal it is for old people to order beds.

Credibility and integrity are eroded as human values are replaced with systems and computerized responses. It's the most efficient way of dealing with the inefficiency and chaos created by those who merely pretend to care for their customers and their people.

In the short term it's more expensive, but in the long term it's more effective if you follow the approach of the incredibly good bosses. They humanize the organization, stressing human values throughout.

Humanity and sensitivity are injected into every conceivable human interface. The managing director personally replies to every complaint. The sales assistant goes out of her way to keep every customer advised on delivery progress. (People forgive delays if they know in advance.) Computerized letters are kept to a minimum. Personal telephone calls are made wherever possible. The immediate boss is forever spending time with her people examining the sensitive interfaces with the customer and how they can continue to get them right. People are taught to 'own' customer problems rather than refer the customer (and the buck) to other departments.

Customer sensitivity becomes a credible reality throughout the organization when every single employee believes and operates in a manner consistent with the customer-service mission.

8

Corporate talk and employee deception

'*Deceiving employees has become a fine art – the art of corporate talk.*'

> 'They put out this glossy annual report which stresses how important employee relations are in the company and how they are taking major strides forward for example on training and development. It's a load of rubbish. I have a hundred staff in my department and my training budget is £1000. For every person £10 per head. Each year for the last three years I've put in for more but they just won't listen. I've got staff who need urgent training – but I've no budget for it.'

Erosion of integrity rots away at the moral fibre of an organization. Employees see the company deceiving the public. Employees know better, know the inadequacies, imperfections and incompetence within the organization. They know that the company carefully hides this from the public gaze. But through a process of corporate talk employees are asked to believe the deception and even articulate it themselves. Many do because it is in their own interest to walk proud under false flags.

Time and time again I come across organizations which, despite the 'excellent employer' guise they put before the public, are infested by poor managers and the consequential low morale of their employees.

Organizations have immense power over the minds of their employees. Much effort is made through corporate communications (I prefer to call it corporate propaganda or corporate talk) to condition the thinking of employees. They are told what to believe. Naïvely, despite a frequent confusion of signals, employees are expected to accept everything their corporate bosses tell them. What they tell them is often censored, dressed up, glossed over and frequently at variance to what they have been told before or deduced for themselves through the informal grapevine. I have come across chief executives who have told managers at a conference that the company has just had its most successful year yet, and then, almost in the same breath that they need to cut costs and work harder because the company is on the brink of survival.

In the end persistent deception through corporate talk undermines credibility, saps morale, erodes integrity and jeopardizes the whole organization.

This corporate talk is often divorced from the real world, a real world in which real people talk a real language which they really understand.

> **'I was impressed with the company before I joined. It all sounded very positive. When they offered me the job they made me three promises. These were that I would receive excellent training, that there would be a regular salary review and that there were superb career prospects. That was fifteen months ago. I haven't received a day's training, my salary is still the same and nobody's talked to me about my career let alone my progress in the job.'**

In their pathetic attempts to talk corporately with employees, corporations often devise a platitudinous language designed not to offend, designed to mean all things to all people. It is the language of motherhood where all things are cosy. Anodyne expression and blandness are the order of the day. It is a language devoid of inspiration and passion – two qualities that make for progress in the real world.

Here is an example:

'Quality, of the highest possible level should be our goal. This means

171

aiming for excellence in the products we manufacture, the services we provide and in every aspect of dealings with the public as well as with colleagues. We should settle for nothing less than the best, aiming to maintain high standards throughout, such that everyone takes a pride in our work.'

It is a deceit. The reality is a company where reception is littered with empty coffee cartons, torn newspapers and disinterested and brusque receptionists. The cardboard boxes in the corridor and the frequent interruptions to meetings give an impression of chaos rather than excellence. The reality is that customers are pestered with invoices they have already paid, that urgent orders are not dispatched 'urgently', that accounts don't liaise with sales, that no one can ever get hold of the personnel executive who is forever up to her eyes in industrial relations problems. It's a reality never reflected in the corporate talk which aims to gloss over the cracks.

Here is another example from an annual report:

'There are many challenges facing us at the moment. The managers and staff who are having to prepare for these changes, and at the same time cope with today's complex problems, are doing so with enthusiasm, intelligence and good humour. The company is fortunate to have a dedicated and talented workforce; and they in turn are fortunate to have a company which is supportive, constructive and practical. It is important for this partnership to continue if we are to achieve our fundamental objectives – the very best in customer service at the right price.'

The difference in this case is that most employees would agree. There is no deceit. The chief executive and his team have made substantial strides forward in employment conditions, in training and development. There has been a tangible and noticeable improvement in the services provided to the customer.

In this case it is possible to relate the 'high level' corporate talk to everyday reality, to changes that have actually taken place. The corporate talk actually has meaning for employees and customers alike.

Therein lies the key. Corporate talk is necessary. By definition top teams need to talk corporately to their public and their employees. By definition they have to talk in a generalized high-level way. However credibility can only be achieved when this corporate talk can be substantiated in the everyday experience of those to whom the corporation is talking.

The unintentional 'fob-off' with soothing words which sound good but have no bearing in practice serve only to reduce the credibility of the top. It generates cynicism all around as people perceive behaviours, decisions and actions totally divorced from the corporate talk.

> 'All we get from the centre is rhetoric. It's never been matched by reality in all the years I've been here. You've only got to look at what they say on pay compared with what they do.'

> 'The biggest thing wrong in this company is the attitude "I'm the boss, therefore I must be right." Put it another way, if you suggest something's wrong they say, "How dare you commit the sin of telling me I'm wrong? There must be something wrong with you even to think that!" They are now involved in this fashionable thing called communications. But it's all downwards. It's all exhortation, you know, expensive videos, posters and badges saying "The company's No 1, so am I!" It's money down the drain. You try to talk to the bosses properly and they don't want to know. They fob you off with waffle. They think they know best, but they know nothing.'

Corporate talk must have meaning. Real meaning in the real world. It must mean something to the telephonist, to the sales assistant, to the floor cleaner as well as to the customer waiting in line.

Incredibly good bosses therefore use a 'chunking-up and chunking-down' process of communications. They chunk up to high-level general statements in order to provide a high-level focus. For example: *'Our aim is to provide the highest possible level of service to our customers.'* They then chunk down to everyday practical examples which inject credibility and meaning into what they are saying. For example: *'We aim to have all telephone calls answered within 5 seconds, all written enquiries responded to within two working days and free coffee available in all our reception areas. All employees represent the company and as such are expected to own customer problems when faced with them.'*

Corporate talk must always be brought alive with the graphics of real committed action, otherwise it risks apparent deceit and degenerates into generality and perceptions of lip-service.

9

Short-term expediency

'Sacrificing the long term in favour of the short term is the biggest cause of credibility loss in any organization.'

Directors delude themselves that they're strategists. They spend months developing grand strategic designs which never get implemented because of short-term pressures and insufficient conviction.

They look fools in the eyes of an all-knowing workforce. Short-term expediency is the most common example of senior executives not practising what they preach, not taking action on their proclaimed words.

I have seen directors declare one minute that 'the company must invest in people as our employees are the assets upon which our long-term success depends' and the next minute slash training budgets in a last-ditch attempt to show a healthy profit in the year.

Directors are forever succumbing to short-term pressures. As a result long-term strategic aims get ignored and yellow with age in filing cabinets. The action always seems to revert to today's cost constraint and tomorrow's profit.

Next year and beyond there might be a shortage of skilled staff, a reducing number of high-calibre managers coming through the system. Next year there might be inadequate premises capacity, a dearth of new products to create the desired market lead. There might be a second-rate systems capability that barely copes with the demands placed upon it today. But next year gets sacrificed for today.

The incredibly good senior executives delegate 'this year' and concentrate on developing an organization fit for next year and beyond. They don't allow themselves to get distracted on today's pay problems, preferring to develop a first-class pay system for next year; they don't get side-tracked on to an in-depth analysis of last week's revenue shortfall, preferring to concentrate on developing the foundation for superb revenue performance two to three years on.

The incredibly good senior executives put their efforts into long-term investment, trusting their superb front-line managers to achieve this quarter's targets. The people getting results today are those they have invested in over the last five years.

It's no good mouthing platitudes about excellent career prospects only to spend two years closing down branch after branch. It's no good trumpeting the launch of a new employee communications programme only to find that everyone's too busy to communicate.

Credibility suffers because senior bosses pretend to be interested in the long term, pretend to be investing in the future, pretend to be putting all these hours into developing grandiose visions and mission statements. But beneath the pretence is a preference for the games children play, a preference for today's actions, today's exciting deeds, today's operational highlights, today's solution to today's problem. Try to get a group of senior executives away for three days to think through long-term strategy. You'll find most of them too busy. At best they'll cram it into a weekend.

Just look at yourself and your own bosses. How much time do you put into today's issues as opposed to next year's? The probability is that next year comes round on a piece of paper, a form to be filled in next month. Strategy becomes a bureaucratic and meaningless exercise which gets lost in detail and never implemented.

Have you ever looked at the strategies you developed five years ago and seen how much influence they've had on today's reality?

If you can honestly say that today's excellent achievements results from the strategic directions your executive team decided upon five years ago then you will be one of the truly few incredible bosses around.

> 'You look back in this organization and you'll find a long trail of unfinished business. Senior management are always throwing balls up in the air. But no one ever catches them, there are so many. It's a way of life here, the bosses like to set things in motion but they don't know how to see them through. There's very little monitoring and control. What's important today is forgotten tomorrow. I think part of the reason is they are all frightened of making mistakes. So they simulate decisiveness and action, they are always making decisions. But there is no follow-through. Very little is achieved in the long run. It's amazing when you think about it.'

There are three keys to long-term strategic success.

The first is to develop a strategic direction which you passionately believe must be achieved. It must be visionary. It must be challenging and it must have a realistic interpretation in terms of pragmatic meaning.

The second is to devote an inordinate amount of time implementing it. This implementation process must begin immediately after the strategy has been adopted and must start with a massive amount of communication and consultation. It is imperative that your passion to achieve this visionary strategy is shared by every single manager and employee.

The third is to avoid getting sucked into day-by-day matters. To that extent you need to discipline yourself to reject trivia from your in-tray as well as develop an incredibly good team you can trust to handle today's operations.

By eliminating short-term expediency and ensuring that your thoughts, words and behaviours are geared to the implementation of a long-term visionary strategy you will increase your credibility and consistently achieve results in the long term.

10

Double-standards

'"It's all right for them, but not for me" is the most commonly practised double-standard in management.'

'He never practises what he preaches. He expects us to be in on time. He even gets upset if we're just five minutes late. Yet come the fourth Friday in every month he goes for his haircut and doesn't get in till 10.00 a.m.'

'They've been pushing performance appraisal at supervisory and middle-management level for two years now. But my director's admitted he's never been appraised himself. Apparently the chief executive hasn't got time for it.'

'It's a joke. She insists on receiving our monthly reports at least five days before the board meeting. She really gets uptight if it's not there on time. But the policy is that she should debrief us within two days of the board meeting. Sometimes she doesn't debrief us at all. Other times she leaves it for a couple of weeks, by which time it's old hat and we've learnt on the grapevine. It's one law for the rich and another for the poor.'

It is incredible how many bosses adopt double-standards, expecting their people to work to higher standards than they practise themselves. There is nothing that diminishes credibility more. People find it galling to see their bosses taking extended lunch-breaks when employees are expected to keep to a strict 45 minutes. People develop resentments when they see their bosses using expenses liberally at the same time as they are constrained to account for every penny.

The lack of consistency in applying key standards leads to confusion, dissent, sloppiness, game-playing and eventual customer dissatisfaction. If a boss is not punctual then the probability is deliveries to customers will not be either.

In the ideal organization there should be one set of standards for all. Everyone is punctual, everyone places a genuinely high priority on communications, everyone gets appraised at least once a year, everyone works to the same expense rules, everyone works the same hours, everyone benefits from corporate success, everyone contributes to the high standards of housekeeping (why wait for the night-cleaner to pick up the empty coffee carton?).

Double-standards erode the integrity of an organization. They arise because many bosses do not think through what their standards are. Without clearly defined standards, practices and behaviours are adopted on a relatively random and perceptual basis.

Superbosses take great trouble to work with their team to evolve an acceptable set of standards to which they can all conform. There is nothing wrong with a casual 'jeans and T-shirt' approach if that is acceptable to all and judged in the best interest of organization performance.

> 'Why should we beat our heads against brick walls, achieving the near impossible when down the road they get away with murder? They have it easy – and get big fat budgets to go with it – that's because they're so inefficient and haven't faced up to some tough decisions. We just get penalized and exploited because we're so good. Expectations of us are much higher than that of the crowd down the road. We are just taken for granted. There are so many double-standards in this company.
>
> 'They take a 5 per cent slice off everyone's budget. It should be nothing off us and 10 per cent off them – they're so inefficient.'

There is nothing wrong in working your own hours, sometimes

at home, sometimes in the office, if that is acceptable to all and judged in the best interests of the customer.

But there is something wrong if a customer cannot get through to a key contact in the organization, if the telephone rings forever, if the promised letter never arrives, if other people in the organization appear disinterested.

To become a credible boss think through your standards today, list them out and discuss them with your team tomorrow. Achieve a consensus that everyone will conform to these standards – and that no double-standards will be tolerated.

11

Alarmism

'Accentuation comes through alarm, exaggeration too.'

> 'The directors will put out a three-line whip to get a so-called urgent report in. We drop everything and we get the report in. Then nothing happens. You hear nothing, nothing happens. You get no feedback. You get the impression the report is totally ignored. I ask my boss and he says, "It's on the agenda of the next meeting." After the next meeting I ask my boss and he says, "We had an urgent problem, we didn't take the item. It got deferred." In the end you give up asking.'

Alarmism is not good management practice, it sends people in all directions, they get out of control.

- Costs go up, alarm bells ring.
- Revenue goes down, alarm bells ring.
- Staff levels are up, alarm bells ring.
- Cash flow is drying up, alarm bells ring.

When the alarm bells ring the unthinking executives begin to spray the organization with exhortations. Urgent meetings are arranged and working parties set up to address the problem. The aim is to create a state of fear in order to force people to reduce costs, increase sales revenue, reduce staff levels and increase cash flow. The reverse happens, of course, but few realize that.

Alarmism rapidly becomes threatening behaviour, which in turn breeds defensiveness and suppression of the truth. The cause of the escalating costs is elsewhere but not in my patch. The revenue is down because of external factors but not because of me. Staff levels are up because of production pressures in the previous half year but not because of my incredibly poor management. It is our customers who are to blame for our cash-flow problems but not me.

The response to the alarm therefore is to induce a 'ducking-and-weaving' process throughout the organization as departmental managers prepare to avoid the oncoming onslaught and protect their own patches.

First time round the alarm might just be effective. Everyone is genuinely scared. So they fight the fire and with great pain and personal sacrifice the costs come down.

The macho bosses at the top, encouraged by the positive response to the alarm, glow with self-satisfaction at the short-term success of their actions. They are, of course, ignorant of the long-term damage these actions inflict. Such macho bosses learn, wrongly, that to achieve an effect they have to create an alarm. Alarmism then becomes the order of the day. The organization lurches from one crisis to another. A large number of managers spend a large part of their time panicking, reacting to the chaos engendered by the frequent alarms.

In responding to the constant state of alarm people's attention gets diverted from the real issues and the real reason they are there. An urgent report on last quarter's revenue shortfall becomes more important than motivating demoralized employees to increase revenue over the next few weeks.

Successful organizations and successful bosses rarely need to press alarm bells. They avoid creating a theatre of fear within which their people perform badly. They convert problems into challenges, crises into learning opportunities. A climate of encouragement and support is developed to meet the challenge, rather than an atmosphere of alarming retribution, rather than a culture of continuing chaos and crisis.

Alarmism is an issue of credibility. There are those rare times when there is genuine cause for alarm. The credible boss takes care to identify the real cause of the problem and then take appropriate action. An incompetent boss will panic into short-term expediency and exhortation as a guise to convince others that he or she is taking positive action.

'Other bosses I found were always panicking. There was always some urgent problem. There was always something that had to be done by the end of the day. It was a question of stopping everything to get it done.

'My new boss is different. He's always calm. Whatever the situation he keeps his cool. He listens carefully and explores the issues with us. He doesn't make excessive demands and never panics, even under pressure.'

You don't have to go far to find alarmism at work. You can list the number of cancelled meetings, delayed responses and difficulties in getting hold of a person due to 'an urgent problem'. Crisis, chaos and alarm become a way of life in many organizations. It effectively becomes an excuse for non-achievement. It enables people to avoid real responsibility for making decisions and achieving things.

The moral is clear, don't ring alarm bells unless you're absolutely convinced there is genuine cause for alarm. And that should only happen, if at all, once every two years.

12

Cover-ups

'Covering up is a blaming disease.'

Fear of blame is the biggest threat to integrity and managerial incompetence.

Success comes from learning. Learning comes from making mistakes. Nobody learns when people seek to apportion blame for mistakes. To avoid blame people cover up and point the finger elsewhere. 'It wasn't me! It was them!' Nobody learns.

Skills deficiencies are covered up too. You'll never find certain people making presentations, or others writing reports. They cover up their inability to present, or to write.

On a larger scale, organizations cover up. They frequently don't 'own up' when things go wrong, when they pollute the river, when faulty wiring leads to a disaster, when an incorrect diagnosis is made.

But one of life's unpalatable truths is that covering up is more unpalatable than the truth. The truth normally emerges and when it does it discredits the person who invented the cover version. Far better to take the credit for learning from an admitted mistake in the first place than being discredited later for failing to expose it.

It doesn't come easy when organization mythology, readily supported by anecdotal evidence, has it that naïve fools who own up lose their promotion prospects and risk their jobs. The prevailing ethos of jungle survival prevails, one covers up.

Furthermore, it is seen as non-supportive to expose the errors of your team to those around. Conflicting principles are at stake. Openness in exposing mistakes conflicts with being supportive in protecting your team from the blaming vultures all around.

The unbelievable truth is that the truth can never be covered up permanently. In the end someone will know. Someone will discover the 'balls-up' on the night shift despite your failure to log it. Someone will discover the administrative 'cock-up' despite your attempt to pass off the sudden flood of customer complaints. And if nobody else discovers it you will discover it on your conscience.

Covering up is endemic in organizations lacking in trust, where open learning is discouraged and where incompetent bosses set themselves up as minor gods who sit in judgement over others. They end up by judging a surfeit of words rather than reality. People cover up reality with words.

Credible bosses rarely rush into blaming others. They are forever reluctant to place value judgements on other people's actions and consequential mistakes. Always giving people the benefit of the doubt they seek to create a learning environment whereby deficiencies, imperfections and mistakes are openly admitted and openly debated without fear of admonition and scorn. They create an environment whereby it becomes credible to be human, to be humble and to admit failings. They avoid creating a threatening environment whereby credibility and dignity are lost by having failings exposed.

'My boss is an expert at snow jobs. He tries to snow us with the impression that everything is all right when we know it isn't. What's worse he tries to snow his director too. The director believes everything in our department is great. If only he knew the truth!'

It is easy to cover up, to tell lies, to be economical with the truth, to make excuses, to avoid the subject, to omit reference to the problem, to duck and weave away from the issue. That is all part of the game in a culture where deviousness and manipulation thrive. But the game inevitably leads to failure because ultimately customers and employees discover the painful reality of the organization's deficiencies.

They lose confidence as the company's integrity and credibility is eroded.

By comparison it takes immense courage to 'own up', to refuse to cover up. In the long term credibility and integrity can only be established through such courage. Such 'owning up' provides a human face to an organization, a human face with which customers and employees can identify, a human face from which everyone can learn. Any short-term erosion of confidence by admitting mistakes can soon be overcome by seizing the opportunity of learning from that mistake.

Covering up will always block such learning opportunities.

13

Guesswork

'Avoiding reality by guessing what's in people's minds is one of the most frequent lapses in integrity.'

A large number of organizations have senior executives who guess at what their employees think. Fearful of what they would find if they actually asked them, they prefer to rely on anecdotes from ingratiating 'yes-men' who've 'bumped into' one or two people in the corridor and as a result can guess at the attitudinal climate in the organization.

It is frightening how top people can get so divorced from the very people, their employees, who are so vital to producing success for the organization.

What people think is often not nice. Even so, what people think influences their performance. If senior executives sense they won't like what their people think then the tendency is to ignore what they think and substitute it with what they think they think. What people think then becomes a guessing game.

Senior executives don't like to think morale is low. So they think it is high even when it's low. If they were to admit it was low this would reflect on their poor leadership, on their bungled decisions, on their insensitivity towards employees. In other words, they would lose credibility. So they don't accept morale is low.

By failing to accept reality, incompetent bosses do nothing about it. At best their guesswork produces half-truths, for example that external factors are to blame for declining sales. What they never discover is the unpalatable reason. This is often poor leadership.

Integrity and credibility collapse as a result. People leave the company in droves and it's always someone else's fault.

It is rare that senior executives set out to find out what their employees really think. They might attempt it half-heartedly by asking their immediate managers, but immediate managers are well trained in giving senior executives the answers they want.

Conversely there are many employees who guess at what their bosses think. People are often fearful of raising certain issues with their bosses, predicting a negative response if they do. In this way, many key issues never get raised with senior management.

Guesswork will always lead to misunderstanding, divisiveness and an alienation which will result in a loss of integrity on the part of the boss.

To achieve credibility it is imperative you clearly establish what your employees think, no matter how distasteful the findings are to you.

14

Negotiating games

'Pay negotiation is alien to good leadership.'

In a competitive world negotiation is essential. In a competitive world everyone is out for the best deal for themselves. If you don't get the deal you want you don't have to make the deal. You can walk away from it. You don't have to sell at a low price. You don't have to buy at a high price.

The error is to believe that managers can negotiate with their own people, their employees. In external negotiation there is no common aim – one party wants a high price, the other a low price. In management there is a common aim. It should be shared between the boss and his or her people. The common aim is to succeed by providing the *best* products and services to the customer. The *best* bosses achieve this by getting the *best* people into their teams and treating them in the *best* possible way. In that way people give of their *best*. There is no room for negotiation in this, no member of the team should lose out on the deal.

Regrettably a tradition has grown up over many decades whereby employees have been forced to negotiate, through powerful trade-union representation, to get the *best* deal from 'big bad bosses' who have historically screwed their people down on pay and conditions.

A ritual has developed whereby the bosses make all the excuses available within their limited repertoire to convince the unions there is little money in the pot whereupon the unions do a war-dance to convince the bosses of their lethal power to damage the organization if the bosses don't conjure more money from the pot (which they invariably do). The bosses' maximum of 4 per cent becomes 5 per cent and the union's minimum of 6 per cent becomes 5 per cent too. As part of the ritual everyone claims victory. The whole process is enshrouded in a mystical aura fostered by so-called expert industrial-relations negotiators who seek to enhance their reputation for tough bargaining and getting the best deal. When the deal is done agreements are set in fudge to facilitate a diverse range of interpretations acceptable to all.

In these ritual negotiating games nobody ever declares the truth. The union cries 'wolf' when there is no wolf. The rich bosses plead poverty when there is no poverty. Horns become locked in public as a demonstration of power whereas behind closed doors the protagonists reach honourable 'nod and wink' agreements over cups of coffee. It would be out of the question for the public to see the unions and the bosses getting on well together, even though in private they quite like each other and there is a lot of common ground.

In the public gaze threat and counter-threat become the order of the day. Reality goes out of the window. At grass roots there is no one to believe. Even if the unions and bosses agree informally in private it is in their vested interests to foster dissent and disagreement publicly. The demonstration of informal agreement would merely serve to erode the power of either side and to invite accusations that 'one is in the pocket of the other'.

These games drain the organization, its bosses and unions of any semblance of integrity and credibility. The other side is always projected as being insensitive, irresponsible, lying, deceitful, disreputable, manipulative, untrustworthy, exploitative, misleading, prejudiced, scare-mongering and many other glib emotional negatives. Objective assessment is discarded as the best bosses are branded as despots and the best union leaders branded as thugs.

You cannot negotiate with people you rely upon. You cannot work together with the competition. Managing for success is all about working together.

You cannot do your *best* for someone who is trying to screw you down. Successful people-management is all about doing your *best* for people so that they can do their *best* for you.

> 'I took over this group of manual workers. They were a difficult group and we got into some trade-union problems. I led the negotiating team with help from personnel but we made little progress. The next thing I know my boss had done a deal with the trade union behind my back. He didn't consult me and if he had I wouldn't have agreed as what he conceded created a long-term rod for my back. He effectively pulled the rug from underneath me. The farce was he had mandated me not to make the concessions he subsequently did. Of course the trade union like him now, they always go to him. But my credibility has gone right down.'

Effective employee relations can never be accomplished through negotiations. It is a lesson many traditional organizations have yet to learn. You cannot negotiate trust, employee care, mutual respect, belief in each other and shared principles. You cannot negotiate harmony, co-operation nor open and honest communication. You cannot negotiate the essentials of effective leadership and team performance. You cannot negotiate what's *best* for your team.

Negotiating games create a climate of distrust and disbelief and as such are the antithesis of integrity and credibility. There is much evidence to suggest that such games ultimately lead to organization failure.

15

'I hear what you say'

'The translation of "I hear what you say" is "I don't want to know! Forget it! I'm not prepared to listen".'

They called it the 'I hear what you say' company. For years the chief executive had been waging a campaign for more effective communications. He said he wanted to know what was going on in the organization, what people thought, what their problems were, what frustrated them. It sounded fine.

So he encouraged his regional directors to set up regular 'communications' meetings with their middle managers. Occasionally he would descend from on high and attend these meetings himself.

They all thought it was a good idea. To begin with the middle managers used these meetings to air their frustrations, concerns and problems. But the only response they received from their regional directors was: 'I hear what you say.' These directors thought that their managers moaned and groaned too much and didn't really appreciate nor understand the pressure the company was under.

And when the chief executive met the regional directors and asked how the monthly communications meetings were going he was told, 'Fine.'

When the chief executive did attend the monthly meetings to learn for himself the managers didn't raise the issues concerning them for fear of embarrassing their regional directors and putting the chief executive on the spot.

After a year or so management morale had become very low. It was always 'I hear what you say' when they raised an issue. Nothing was ever done about their concerns because it was perceived that they were negative and belly-achers.

In reality nobody ever heard what the managers said. Their concerns were effectively dismissed every time they were raised.

It didn't occur to the chief executive nor the regional directors that by attempting to promote effective communications through monthly meetings that they were diminishing their own credibility and eroding integrity by failing to listen and learn at these meetings. The communications campaign had become no more than a façade.

To achieve credibility you have to really mean what you say and do something about what you hear.

16

Papering over the cracks

'Substituting paper systems for real people management is one of the biggest integrity gaps in many organizations today.'

'First it was OVA (overhead value analysis), then it was MMT (monthly management targets). Next came PCC (personal career counselling) and this was quickly followed by WBG (weekly briefing groups). Soon after came PRA (performance review and assessment). Next on the list was BPC (business planning cycle) and then there was CSE training (customer service excellence). Now we're back to ZBA (zero based analysis) as we prepare for CCM (cost centre management) and PIP (profit improvement plans). Most of these initiatives have come from CERT (chief executives review team) in conjunction with SESG (senior executives support group). Rumour has it they intend to establish a new approach through SDRG (service delivery review groups) and SDT (strategy development teams).

'All this in two years. It's one fashion after another, one flavour of the month followed by another. It hasn't made any difference at all to the bottom line and our bosses are still useless!'

The paper might be a performance appraisal form, a management by objectives (MBO) worksheet, a briefing note, a career planning schedule or a wide variety of other bureaucratic employee development practices.

The truth is often unpalatable and can cause extreme discomfort, especially when confronted face to face. Incredibly bad bosses avoid it and then simulate it bureaucratically under a pretence of 'open and honest' management. To do so they use artificial systems such as performance appraisal, MBO and staff development reviews.

There is nothing wrong with such systems if they are meaningful and tackle the truth up-front.

Regrettably these systems too often become a flimsy façade for effective management. Organizations are deluded to believe that managers who complete these forms are effective, whereas many effective managers see the form-filling as a bureaucratic chore that gets in the way of real management.

Persuading a poor manager to complete an appraisal form will not make that manager any better, whereas the best managers will not necessarily need the form in their regular appraisals of individuals in the team.

Persuading poor managers to complete an MBO worksheet will not make those managers achieve their objectives. Competent managers achieve their objectives without the imposition of an MBO system.

Persuading poor managers to use the company briefing system will not improve their communications. At best they'll lean on it as a crutch. Superbosses communicate regularly and effectively without the need of briefing systems.

Such paper-systems for managing people achieve little. At best they reinforce a management culture which values the provision of feedback to employees, the setting of objectives and regular two-way communication. At worst they conflict with a prevailing culture where managers don't care to communicate, don't bother to set objectives nor advise employees on the progress they're making.

Imposition of a bureaucratic system of leadership will never change attitudes in the direction required. Unless the prevailing management attitude can be developed to apply positively the underlying principles of the system then managers will simply manipulate the system. For example managers will use performance appraisal as an excuse to delay dealing with difficult 'people' issues for up to a year. And managers will use MBO to set meaningless and artificial objectives to ensure that they get a good rating in twelve months' time (and thus a good pay rise).

> **'My boss came in to appraise me. It was the first time I'd seen him for six weeks. He normally leaves me to do my own thing. He hates appraisals but was doing it because the chief executive insisted. It was the most debilitating experience I'd ever had. I felt like resigning there and then. He didn't know what he was talking about. He had no idea of the work I'd been doing and he just waffled on, inventing comments which made no sense at all. I couldn't understand what it was all about. It was unbelievable!'**

There are other dangers too when organizations introduce paper systems for leading people. Thus many personnel departments attempt to give these systems credibility with the pretext that they are scientific. For example 'performance rating systems' abound when it comes to appraisal. In one company every single employee was regularly appraised and rated. The average rating was 7/10. On being challenged about what 7/10 meant the personnel manager said, 'Above average.' This was despite the fact that company revenues were declining and profits on a downward trend. In other words the *average* appraisal rating was *above average* in a *below average* company! Such systems and the people who use them can have no credibility.

These systems often become pseudo-scientific mechanistic appeasement (or persecution) processes which by-pass the intended task of objectively measuring performance and providing constructive feedback and advice on improvement opportunities.

These processes will merely serve to undermine the credibility and integrity of a manager as he or she concocts diplomatic words to keep the employee happy.

Deficiencies in performance are incredibly difficult to confront.

Attempting it once a year by conducting a formal appraisal is not necessarily the best way.

Similarly high performance is incredibly difficult to recognize and appreciate. It often becomes confused with high levels of activity, bright personality and positive attitudes. Furthermore, attempts to recognize success only once a year is hardly motivating.

Formalizing performance measurement and feedback by means of a bureaucratic process enables incredibly poor bosses to distance themselves from the everyday task of performance assessment. Such bosses become confused between behaviour and achievement, between attitude and results, between aptitude and success. They become deceived by their own limited and unchallenged perceptions. They merely guess at the measure. The end result is frequently bland, boring and sterile, an appraisal form completed annually which has little meaning or relevance.

Successful bosses don't need bureaucratic processes to manage people properly. They will use the system if it genuinely helps, but discard it if it gets in the way of an open, honest and caring approach to employee motivation. If there is a performance

---

'The bosses I've respected in the past are those that seem to know what they're all about. They got on with the job, believed in themselves and their people, they had clarity of purpose, and they knew how to take their people with them. They didn't need all these new-fangled people management systems to help them out.

'Nowadays it's different. All I seem to be doing is fighting the company – in trying to do the job the company wants me to do. The bosses don't understand. They introduce all these devices, like MBO and performance appraisal because they say things need to change. And when you've completed the MBO worksheet and performance appraisal form they shout "Great! Things have changed, haven't we been clever?"

'They ignore the real problems. They play at inventing self-fulfilling prophecies.'

---

problem they will confront it on the spot rather than wait for the annual round of appraisals.

Competent bosses actually *do want* to set objectives, *do want* to provide feedback on performance, *do want* to advise on career issues, *do want* to spend a lot of productive time on two-way communications. What they don't want is an enforced system to do what are essentially good people-management practices.

It is the incompetent bosses who hide behind the paper-systems to avoid dealing with people.

These systems were designed to get bad bosses to adopt good practices. In reality they remain bad bosses by using the system as a substitute for good management.

17

Carrot pay

'The myth of carrot and stick remains entrenched among those who believe in performance-related pay.'

You may as well call it carrot pay. It is one of the wildest examples of how organizations corrupt their culture.

Basic management training, first year, teaches you that the 'carrot-and-stick' approach to motivating people for high performance is the least effective. The theories of Maslow, McGregor, Herzberg and Likert rely on a deeper understanding of the complexities of the human condition than on the simplistic presumption that carrots motivate.

Yet amazingly, in the early 1990s, top bosses who have probably never received any basic management training, are rushing to follow the fashion by installing pay schemes based on carrot and stick motivation.

Performance-related pay cracks open the integrity of an organization, creating immense divisions and inequities between its people. The consequence is the reverse of that intended. Demotivation and low morale set in as 75 per cent of the population recoil from the perceived injustice of receiving an average or below merit award while a few lucky people, the minority 25 per cent, receive above average awards as a result of some scarcely objective assessment.

Subjectivity reigns in the world of carrots. It is impossible to differentiate fairly between the performance of all individuals in a

> 'There was a letter on my desk when I arrived back in the office after a long overseas trip. It was open for all to see. It simply read, "After careful consideration the company has decided that your performance does not warrant a merit increase this year." It was word-processed and nobody had bothered to sign it. It came from the director of personnel. I just blew up! Having been away on business for two weeks, having sacrificed weekends and evenings to help the company – as frequently happens – and this was all the thanks I got.'

team. The few exceptional people are there for all to see. They are the ones who get promotion in due course. Meanwhile they, like the rest, are best rewarded in accordance with market forces.

At the other end of the performance spectrum you cannot dangle carrots in front of poor or average contributors and hope for meritorious performance. Money is no substitute for management. If it is allowed to become so there will be a major lapse of integrity. By introducing carrot pay top bosses opt out of the essential leadership role of inspiring their people to achieve great things.

If possible you should select the best people, pay them the highest salary in the market-place and work flat out to help them achieve great results.

18

Self-entertainment

'It takes a strong person to resist indulging in self-entertainment.'

Whether you are chief executive or floor-cleaner, work can be tedious. For the chief executive there is the never-ending in-tray, innumerable calls to be made and the same old problems which seem to recur year after year. Draft budgets are always too high, revenue projections are always too low. Managers are always demanding more resources, efficiency always has to be improved and year by year the competition seems to become even more intense. From time to time it seems like a nightmare.

For the floor-cleaner it is the same old dirty floors day in day out. People never seem to bother. Coffee cartons are thrown everywhere, fag-ends overflow from ash-trays, people shoot crumpled paper at waste-baskets and miss. They all have dirty feet and coffee is invariably spilled on the walkways. Who cares?

Well, floor-cleaners do. They take a pride in getting the floors spotless every evening, but never ever do they get a word of thanks or appreciation. Everybody seems to take them for granted. From time to time it seems like hell.

Chief executives have their escape. It may be on the golf course where they delude themselves that the best deals are struck, or in the cocoon of their chauffeur-driven cars *en route* to the club, or having a relaxing three-hour lunch with one of their major customers whom they regard more as a friend. Or it may be in the box at the opera, or on a first-class flight to Hong Kong for a sales promotion. (They rarely get time to attend the sales promotions in Birmingham.)

They will always deny it. They will always say they hate all this travel and entertainment. They will always say they only do it because it's absolutely necessary. But in reality they are escaping through the process of self-entertainment. If only they would admit it they would retain some credibility. After all it's only human to indulge once in a while, isn't it?

Cleaners have relatively little opportunity for escaping through self-entertainment. At least they get free coffee in the staff room.

The credibility gaps arise because the more senior you are in the organization the more opportunity you have to manipulate the organization and its budgets in favour of meeting your own selfish needs for escape and entertainment.

At board level it is the company that pays for a champagne reception at the home of the chief executive. In the view of the chief executive it is absolutely essential for profit. It isn't. Floor-cleaners don't need champagne to clean floors. Nor do customers need it to purchase the company's products.

Senior executives diminish their credibility by justifying all entertainment as essential for business. But normally there is no justification. It's self-entertainment. So recognize it and be honest about it.

19

Mindless memos

'People write memos because they can't find time for people nor face up to them.'

MEMO TO: ALL GRADE 3 MANAGERS

I am appalled to find that despite my memo of 15th January your supervisors are still allowing certain ...

'Every time I went to see my boss about a problem he wrote a memo to other people afterwards saying I'd raised this problem. I felt really bad about it, I was really embarrassed. So I don't go to see my boss now.'

Memos are less than efficient. They create inconceivable tensions throughout an organization.

MEMO TO ALL STAFF

As a result of our messenger boy being mugged while bringing cash back from the bank I have decided to withdraw the facility whereby staff can cash cheques on a Friday afternoon.

Memos are cheap, nasty forms of communications.

Receiving memos can be like having cold water squirted in your face.

> **MEMO TO ALL DEPARTMENT MANAGERS, RIVERSDALE**
>
> **The Chief Executive will be visiting Riversdale on Thursday, 20th June. Last time he came he commented adversely about staff drifting back late from lunch and also that the staircases at the back of the building had not apparently been cleaned for some time. Please ensure this does not happen again. I will be asking my Assistant to personally ensure that ...**

By looking someone in the eyes you have the opportunity to validate what a person is saying. The eyes tell you whether the person means it or not.

Bosses who have no backbone, who are devoid of much principle and low on integrity, avoid looking people in the eyes. They generate memos instead as a guise for fast, efficient communication. Their excuse is that face-to-face communication is time-consuming, that a simple dictate typed by a secretary and copied to ten people is far more efficient. But a simple memo dictate can be the subject of ten or more different interpretations. So people gather together in corners exchanging interpretations, guessing at what the boss really meant – or was getting at. After all, the art of political diplomacy is to say things indirectly. Directness offends. So people have to guess at the underlying meaning of the memo, at what the boss is trying to say with his or her exhortative screed.

When things get out of control more paper is generated. Forms are created as a bureaucratic, albeit ineffective, way of restoring control. Memos are written calling for more reports – ostensibly to call people to account. But reports can be fudged and in any event soon become redundant.

The only way to establish trust, credibility and integrity is to face up to the difficult question by looking someone in the eyes and asking, 'Why?' 'Why was that report so late?' 'Why did we let that customer down?' 'Why has our new recruit been looking so miserable lately?' 'Why do you always seem to be so negative?'

Those who lead to succeed always tackle the difficult issues head on by face-to-face contact and by looking people in the eyes. The worst bosses merely avoid the eye contact and generate paper instead.

> 'I think talking has gone out of fashion since our new director arrived. I now receive between 20 and 30 memos a day. The director writes memos to my boss and copies me, my boss then writes his interpretation to me and copies the director. I rarely see either of them, they are too busy writing memos.'

> 'She was a bad boss. Very personable but she could never confront difficult issues. She'd get round them by hiding behind ambiguous memos. You had to guess between the lines what she really meant.'

Memos undermine credibility because they erode understanding, erode relationships, erode confidence and trust, erode openness and honesty, and intrinsically erode the moral fibre of an organization. Incredibly good bosses value their people so much that they invariably communicate face to face, or personally by telephone.

Five minutes of eye-ball to eye-ball contact can save vast reams of paper.

MEMO TO ALL STAFF

'Don't write memos.'

20

Information games

'Information is power, a perverse power, people play games with it.'

If you have vital information and no one else does, you perceive yourself to be in a position of power. As soon as everyone has that information you become powerless. But if you hold on to vital information the probability is that no one will know you have it, no one will know how powerful you are. So to enhance your credibility you leak out information to confidants; in this way you hope to preserve as well as enhance your power. But, of course, your confidants have their own confidants.

With information you have the ability to play games with people, to demonstrate that you know more than them, to spring surprises on them, to catch them out, to get them on the defensive. You have information that things aren't working out in someone else's patch. That information gives you power – the power to enhance your own credibility and diminish that of others. When there is information that things have gone wrong in your own patch then you have the power, you think, to withhold it from those who might attack you.

As a senior boss you might well be privy to information which has a bearing on people down the line. People down the line know this. Therefore it pays them to defer to you, to manoeuvre themselves into your confidence. They know that if there is a major re-organization, or a senior-level resignation, or major changes about to take place, that you have the power to withhold this information, forcing them into the humiliation of finding out on the grapevine, or, what's worse, through a formal notice.

The first to get to the 'hot' information is the person who enhances his or her credibility by being the first to release it into the grapevine.

By withholding information you have the ability to constrain your enemies from working effectively, to mislead your boss – if that suits your end and to manipulate your people. But you deceive yourself if you believe you are enhancing your own credibility.

You will be seen for what you are: a person without integrity.

Some bosses are so incompetent they don't play with information, they just don't bother about it, inadvertently withholding it in an almost total failure to communicate. Such bosses frequently cause chaos, their people never knowing what's going on, never having enough information to do their jobs effectively.

Other bosses use information as a delaying tactic, asking for more and more in order to delay making a decision.

Successful leaders establish a climate of trust. In such a climate there are few secrets, perhaps only those of a very personal and intimate nature. In such a climate there is a free flow of information. There are no restrictions. There is no need to withhold because there is confidence that credibility is not established through the possession of information, but by a measure of achievement. People trust that they will be the first to be told if there is a re-organization that affects them or if there is a senior-level resignation.

> 'They [senior management] fob off decisions by asking for more information. We sweat our guts out getting the information they ask for. When we present it they don't believe it, they pick holes in it. We never get anywhere with them.'

Superbosses soon learn that the grapevine works with incredible speed and with an incredible ability to distort information. They therefore put much effort into 'beating' the grapevine and gossip-machine by ensuring that the right people get the facts first.

Often this requires meticulous planning and sophisticated logistics. Nothing diminishes the credibility of a boss more than failing to tell subordinates something he or she believes they should know. Credible bosses are sensitive to this and go out of their way to ensure this does not happen. Effective communications is therefore always at the forefront of their minds and they are prepared to devote a lot of time to it.

Credible bosses empower their people by the effective dissemination of vital information.

21

Internal politics

'*More organizations are diseased by internal politics than their bosses dare to admit.*'

Failure to pursue integrity within an organization creates a void filled by destructive internal politics.

In the absence of secure trusting relationships people rapidly develop perceptions of enemies within the organization. Survival is perceived as a process of poisoning the enemy, through innuendo, and ingratiating oneself with those in power.

The organization becomes corrupt with a diffusion of warring inner circles and informal lobbying systems bereft of any integrity. Words become more important than action. Action becomes more important than achievement. The unprincipled boss, either unaware of or even party to such political manoeuvres, is deceived by a plethora of opinion conforming to his or her view and a dearth of counter-argument. At best lip-service is given to contrary opinion.

The pursuit of integrity creates trusting relationships which obviate the need for internal politics, creates an environment where the frank exchange of opinion results in a vitality and degree of organization health best suited for high performance.

High priority and much time will be needed to facilitate lively debates where there are no restrictions on the agenda, no holds barred and where criticism is levelled as a genuine means of achieving improvement.

Eliminating internal politics means a total lack of toleration, on the part of the boss, of all 'muck-spreading' indirect criticism, all 'yes-boss' ingratiation and any other manoeuvring.

> 'Nobody takes any risks in this organization any longer; they are all too busy watching their backs. You learn the hard way that you've got to keep your head below the parapet. If something goes wrong they pin it on to the person closest to the problem at that moment. There's too much scapegoating going on. The bosses don't support you, they seize on the opportunity to discipline you to prove their virility. We've had too many sacrificial lambs round here. The bosses won't take responsibility, they just push blame downwards. The lower ranks know it, they are not paid for all this accountability, it frightens them. So in the end they do nothing but protect themselves from exposure. If you don't the whole weight of the organization comes down against you.'

Nine out of ten organizations I come across are riddled with internal politics. Job interest seems secondary to the latest rumour of head-chopping and blood-letting. Energies and times are deployed in gossip and back-biting. In the tenth organization there is a calm air of excitement as everyone, trusting one another, directs their attention to achieving the vision of success to which they are all committed.

Internal politics are the antithesis of integrity.

22

Patronage

'Patronage is never objective. It is based on perceptions of superiority.'

The illusion is that credibility, self-fulfilment and success is derived from the establishment of superiority and that this is best achieved by making out others to be less superior. Not necessarily inferior, but perhaps 'junior' or 'needing help'.

Patronage reinforces the ego, fulfils the occasional basic instinct to be good, to be kind. Patrons are made to feel important. Ingratiation becomes the norm.

The danger is that one patronizes the people who want the security and comfort of patronage – the very people who should never be patronized. And the very people who should be patronized – those dynamic up-and-coming people who have a mind of their own, who question everything, challenge the system and even speak up are those who rarely receive patronage.

Patronage is prevalent in modern management. Despite all the formal and quasi-objective personnel processes the favoured ones always tend to come to the surface – to receive their favours. Without patronage favoured causes would become lost causes. Without patronage those promoting the cause fail. Causes do not speak for themselves, and those speaking for them need support from above.

Through patronage objective assessment of people and causes is discarded in favour of a cosmetic reality whereby managers play games in pursuit of the support of their senior executives. The game is not to present the cause objectively but to present yourself in the best possible light as the embodiment of worthy causes. Worthy causes like training, improved communications, greater investment in systems, more emphasis on marketing, a better corporate identity, a fresh approach to PR or a re-organization.

Writing a cold, two-dimensional report on these issues achieves little. Written recommendations often mean little and are often ignored. It is people that support causes, not paper. The trick therefore is not to write more reports but to secure personal patronage for the cause from one of the power-brokers within the narrow circle of influence at the top.

While patronage is necessary in any organization the problem lies in the subjective application of the patron's powers.

If you passionately believe that a 'cause' should be promoted it is quite proper for you to seek patronage for that cause from the upper echelons of the organization. A credibility gap arises when there is an attempt to pretend that the decision was not made under 'patronage' but objectively following a careful analysis of all the options.

Patronage is quite healthy when it openly aims to help a person promote a worthy cause. It is less healthy when it merely seeks to help a person the patron likes at the expense of people he or she doesn't like. It is also unhealthy when bosses use patronage to demonstrate their own superiority over what they see as inferior juniors. Requiring help and support should never imply inferiority. 'To patronize' has a negative connotation because of the implication of superiority.

Superbosses act as patrons for the great ideas produced by their teams and for those sparkling young individuals who need a lot of encouragement to transform their creative energies into a profitable performance.

In fact the greatest patron is the humble boss.

23

Disbelieving bosses

'Acting on belief can require courage.'

When you don't agree with your seniors or don't believe the reasons they give you, yet have to implement their decisions, then you encounter tremendous threats to your own integrity.

Acting against belief is easy. You merely compromise your principles and do what you are told. You become a 'disbelieving boss'. Why try to implement decisions you don't believe in? If you don't believe the decision why should your people? You might act out a role of appearing to accept the board's crazy decision but in the end your people will 'suss' you out, will discover that you are acting without conviction, without belief. After all your front-line people have very sensitive antennae. Whatever you say and however you say it they will know that you are against the decision made by your superiors. They will know you don't approve and are implementing it against your will. They will be right to question your integrity. Your credibility will plummet.

Yet the terrible reality is that you can never agree with all the decisions the board makes. There are going to be times when you become a 'disbelieving boss' no matter how hard you try to toe the party line. Resignation is only a solution on major issues of principle. The vast majority of decisions you don't believe in are minor. You are therefore taught to compromise. But you are forever compromising your principles.

There is a solution. It requires immense integrity. You have to differentiate between the decision and the reason. If you accept your boss's authority then you have to accept his or her decision.

But you don't have to accept his or her reasons. (The only time you wouldn't accept the decision is when it compromises a key principle which you personally hold with great conviction.) Having accepted the decision but not the reason you can be honest with your people as well as yourself. You say to your team, 'I don't agree with the reasons behind the board's decision but I respect their judgement. I could well be wrong and they could well be right. I accept that they are in a position of authority and will do everything to help them implement the decision.'

Honesty pays. It always does. It means being true to yourself and to your people. As soon as you go around saying you believe when you don't believe you will suffer a major lapse in credibility.

The board for all its worth, and you in your own way as a boss, should always be reluctant to place its subordinates in a position of prospective insubordination. The aim must always be to take your people with you, to get them to accept both the decision and the reason. This requires immense powers of toleration, patience and understanding, as well as much time. The dividend is great. In the due process of time, in the due process of debate, consultation and involvement, the best decisions will normally emerge, decisions acceptable to most.

'I didn't believe what my director was telling me about the reason for closing down the unit. He instructed me to inform my people there. They are a great team, have worked for me for years. When I told them I could see the disbelief in their eyes. They just couldn't believe it. I felt my own credibility was severely diminished for communicating a decision I didn't believe in.'

The incredibly bad bosses take the worst possible route. They often impose decisions without giving reasons. It is virtually impossible to believe in such bosses. They lack credibility because they give no credible reasons.

Ideally to achieve anything you must believe in what you're doing. 'Disbelieving bosses' in the end achieve less than believing bosses. That's why competence is a function of credibility.

Part 5

TEN STEPS

In this final part of the book ten key steps are outlined which should be taken if one wants to become an *incredible boss* who achieves great success with integrity and credibility.

●

The steps derive from all the previous sections in this book.

●

Consider each step carefully and relate them to your own personal management situation.

Step 1

Self-starting

'Incredibly successful bosses start with themselves. The first step therefore is to ask yourself honestly: "Am I really a self-starter?"'

Self-starters do not wait for luck, knowing they might wait for ever. Nor do they wait for their organization, knowing that organizations appear almost static in the way they move. Self-starters create the opportunities and the circumstances for their future success. It is a negative condition of the human mind to believe that only a lucky few can be successful. Everyone has the potential to be successful. All it requires to start with is a realistic, challenging and achievable definition of future success.

Self-starting involves an exciting process of self-exploration by which one rediscovers one's talents, reconfirms one's beliefs and redevelops an ambitious vision of success.

Self-starting means starting now to re-evaluate one's position and contribution to the organization. It means taking some positive and possibly painful steps to establish the level of one's integrity and credibility in the eyes of others.

Self-starting means a fresh start every day, learning constantly by frequent appraisal of one's own behaviours, actions, words, beliefs and relationship with others.

Self-starting means taking on accountability for all results, determinate or indeterminate, negative or positive, *en route* to one's vision of success.

Self-starters do not apportion blame to others who appear to block their success or cause their failure. Self-starters do not blame circumstances outside their control, nor bad luck. Self-starters never use excuses.

Self-starters look to the inside to determine the outside. Those who fail are those who look to the outside to determine the inside.

Self-starters come to terms essentially with themselves and in this way come to terms with the world. Self-starters know what they are potentially capable of (which is normally much more than they think). They therefore pursue what others fear to pursue. They achieve the near impossible knowing that without their vision of it it would be impossible.

Self-starters manage to self-start the teams they work with, unleashing talents and potential individuals in the team never thought they had, creating goals the team never thought they could attain. Self-starters, in coming to terms with their own limitations, exceed them.

Integrity starts with yourself, whereas credibility is the world's reflection of it. As soon as you've made the personal commitment to start with yourself you can take the next step of looking honestly at yourself. First and foremost, are you really honest as a manager?

Step 2

Honesty rating

'To become an incredibly successful boss it is essential that you are totally honest with yourself as well as with your people.'

The second step therefore is to rate yourself on 'honesty' as a boss on the following scale (see Table 2). There is no magic about this, in fact all it requires is asking yourself a very straightforward question and being totally honest in answering. The question of course is: *how honest are you?*

Checkpoints before you rate yourself

- Are you always honest with your assistant/deputy/secretary about his or her capabilities and limitations?

- Are you always honest with members of your team about their performance?

- Are you always honest with your boss about your thoughts – especially about him or her, or do you keep many of your thoughts to yourself?

- Do you always check what you are saying for honesty?

- Do you often modify what you say to other people to make it more palatable and acceptable?

The minute-by-minute test of your capability as a leader will now depend on ensuring that you can increase your level of honesty in everything you say and do at work.

Table 2 Honesty rating

Which paragraph most applies to you?	Honesty rating
My conscience is clear, I am totally honest in everything I say and do as a boss. I am also honest with my boss. I constantly seek the truth about myself. My people are totally honest with me.	10
I struggle to be honest at work, but occasionally have to use 'ploys' to achieve my desired ends. There are occasions when I cannot be honest with my people, nor they with me.	7
I cannot be completely honest with my people. If I were, there would be a reaction as they would not understand. I am not sure how honest they are with me. So I am always modifying what I say to people, and modifying what I hear.	5
I have found it rarely pays to be honest with people at work. I keep my cards close to my chest and only let on what I think to one or two people who are close confidants. I don't believe my boss is honest with me either.	3
I've learnt that people are never honest with me. They pretend to be but in the end invariably let me down. So I do my own thing. It's a rat race. To be honest with people would be suicide.	0

WARNING: Honesty is an absolute! It cannot be achieved all the time.

For people to believe you it will be necessary that your honesty be backed up by a clear set of beliefs and values. The next step therefore is to clarify your beliefs and values and this is dealt with in the following section.

Step 3

Confirmation of beliefs and values

'No matter how honest you strive to be, your credibility as a successful leader will not be attained unless you articulate and adhere to a clear personal philosophy of management.'

Your next big step as a leader therefore is to clarify, challenge and thus confirm the beliefs and values you personally hold.

You should be able to relate all the management decisions you take to these beliefs and values.

To do this, take a blank sheet of paper and prepare a brief statement of your beliefs and values. Each belief and value should be illustrated with a practical application in your day-by-day task as a leader.

Some examples to stimulate your thinking are given in Table 3 overleaf. This table does not contain an exhaustive list of beliefs and values. They are examples provided by the author. It is more important that the reader develops and clarifies his or her own set of beliefs.

REMEMBER:
Your integrity and credibility as a leader will be measured by the way your everyday behaviour and actions conform with your professional beliefs and values.

Table 3 Clarification of beliefs and values

Belief	Value statement	Example of practical application
1 Caring	I believe in genuinely caring for my team	I will take time out to console the juniors in the team after the setback on their project
2 Honesty	I constantly strive to be honest with my people and my boss	Tough as it is, I will see my boss and be honest with him about the mistake I made in promoting the young woman from marketing
3 Pay	I believe in paying my people the best and do not believe in performance-related pay	I will go and chase personnel to get the regrading through for our senior clerical people. I will seek a meeting with my boss and personnel to put my view about performance-related pay
4 Performance appraisal	I believe it is critical to give feedback to my team (and I don't believe it's necessary to wait for personnel to send round the appraisal form)	I wasn't impressed with the account manager's presentation to our dealers. I will take her aside and give her some helpful feedback. I won't wait until November when personnel send round the appraisal form
5 Involvement	While I believe the ultimate decision is mine, I do believe in involving my people in the process of making decisions	We have a difficult decision coming up with one of our suppliers. I will involve my team and seek their guidance as they are directly affected
6 Vision	I believe it crucial to have a clear vision of where my department is going over the next year	I will set aside an afternoon with my team to review our departmental vision

Table 3 (cont.)

Belief	Value statement	Example of practical application
7 Listening	I believe it should be high priority to spend time listening to people in the department and finding out what they think	I will set up a series of open forum sessions with small groups of staff in the department to provide them with an opportunity to air any points they want to make
8 Training	I place great value on having highly trained staff	I will resist pressures from my boss to take one of our high-flyers off the supervisors' course because we are so short-staffed
9 Trust/ delegation	I really value the contribution my team make and trust that they will make the best decisions possible	I will send my deputy to Japan on my behalf. It will be his first experience of negotiating a major deal by himself, but I trust he'll get it right
10 Fun	I place a lot of value on my team enjoying their work	Last month was the best ever in revenue terms. It was hard work but great fun. This month will be even better. We'll arrange a fun evening at the local club. There will be champagne for all
11 Thanks	I put a lot of value in recognizing, appreciating and rewarding a good job done	I will continue to go out of my way to identify superb work done by members of the team and to express appreciation for it
12 Risks	I don't believe there is any 'no-risk route' to success. I believe I have to let my people take a few risks from time to time	I'm not too sure about the team's proposal for a further initiative in the South East but I'll take a flyer and support them

Having clarified your own beliefs and values it is important that you frequently challenge them and confirm them.

The danger is that the beliefs become fixed and that you take it for granted you are putting them into practice.

Most bosses, for example, believe in giving thanks for a good job done. It frequently comes as a surprise to them therefore when they discover, somewhat too late, that their people are demotivated because they don't feel their contribution is appreciated.

Other bosses believe that they are excellent communicators. It comes as a great shock when they learn that their people see them differently, that their people feel their bosses never let them know what's going on.

There are few bosses who would claim to be other than honest. But many of their people think otherwise, claiming that their bosses are less than honest with them.

In this day and age the majority of bosses believe in doing the best for their staff. But there are still large groups of staff who don't see it this way, who think their bosses are mean-minded and screw them down.

There are numerous other examples, cited in the rest of this book, whereby bosses do not practise what they preach, whereby they take it for granted that they are seen the way they want to be seen.

To achieve great integrity and credibility it is essential that you constantly challenge your beliefs and values. They should never become fixed. If they do they can develop into dogma and rhetoric. Beliefs and values should be evolutionary. Honesty, for example, is a simple enough concept, but the meaning of it evolves through a lifetime of experience.

Similarly, as beliefs and values acquire new meanings it is important to challenge yourself on the application of them. A child is taught to say 'thank you' when she is offered an apple. She is not taught to express appreciation for all the other things her parents do for her. It is only later in life that the phrase 'thank you' takes on the meaning of appreciation. Such is the evolutionary process.

To become an incredible boss it is therefore important to take the step of regularly clarifying, challenging and confirming your own beliefs and values.

Step 4

Establishing a vision of success

'Those incredibly rare bosses who succeed have a vision of success founded on the highest levels of integrity and credibility.'

The next step is to establish a vision to which everyone in your team and throughout the organization can commit. The secret is belief. It is imperative, if you wish to be successful, that you have a personal vision of success which you passionately believe must be achieved.

Strategic goals, long-term objectives, are meaningless without such passion and belief.

But a vision of success is more than a set of strategic goals. It is not easy to articulate and communicate strategic goals. Frequently they lack colour, are devoid of feeling and are rendered meaningless by being expressed in generalized high-level statements.

Superbosses inject graphic meaning into their vision with the aim of ensuring every single employee knows what it means in terms of his or her own vital contribution to the attainment of the vision. Without such meaning, without such belief the vision becomes a mere slogan. It will lack credibility and acceptance within the organization. Without real meaning there can be no real commitment.

The vision itself must be articulated in a simple way that can be understood by everyone and interpreted by them in terms of pragmatic action. However, should the boss start behaving, speaking, deciding and acting in a way which is inconsistent with the achievement of the vision, then the vision itself will be devalued. It will become undermined, debased and end up as a mere exhortative slogan to which people pay lip-service only. When employees observe their bosses neglecting the very vision they themselves set, why should employees do otherwise? Such is the erosion of integrity. The basis of the vision must have real value to all in the organization.

The challenge is to establish a vision which you believe must be achieved and which you believe will not be undermined by your own behaviours, words, actions and decisions. Success cannot come without a vision of that success. As such, success is inextricably linked to integrity and credibility.

It is a constant challenge. A day should not go by without your examining your own behaviour and actions in relation to the vision you seek to achieve.

You cannot establish a vision of success, document it and forget about it and then review it with the team after six months – in the mean time getting on with the 'real' work. That will merely undermine the meaning and value of the vision. In too many organizations the establishment of the mission is seen to be peripheral to the mainstream of the business. The mission becomes marginal, something to be tacked on to a manager's duties when he or she has a spare afternoon.

Progress towards achieving a vision of success must embrace the day-by-day work of everyone in the team. All resources, all effort, all energy, all thought, all tasks, all decisions, all actions must be geared to the achievement of that vision.

In other words, the work you do every day must be an integral part of the progress you make in achieving the vision. Guiding your team towards this achievement is intrinsically your job as a boss.

In fact everything that happens within your area of responsibility must be part of an organic evolution towards achieving the vision. Today's step therefore is to begin that challenging process of establishing a vision of success for your area.

Step 5

Determining levels of integrity

'You can philosophize for ever about the meaning of integrity, but unless customers and employees alike perceive you as having the highest integrity then you are likely to fail.'

You are the company and so are your people. It's you the boss who have overall management accountability for all the interfaces between customers and employees. Step 5 therefore is to check your vision and beliefs for emphasis on integrity with customers and employees.

1. Determining levels of integrity with customers

To sustain integrity with customers the company's approach to them must constantly be challenged, debated and studied. You will need to examine carefully all types of feedback from customers as well as take new initiatives in this respect. The key questions in your mind all the time should be:

- 'Are we doing our best for our customers, is there any evidence that we are letting them down?'

- 'Am I personally honest with customers and employees?'

- 'Do our customers trust us to supply the high quality of services and products we say we will?'

To achieve the high standards required for long-term success it is essential that all employees develop a positive attitude towards sustaining the company's integrity with its customers. This will necessitate placing a high value on training courses, induction videos, talks by senior company executives as well as articles in the company's newspaper.

The pursuit of customer integrity needs the highest possible profile internally if it is ever to be achieved; it also needs to become part of the routine daily challenge for everyone in the business. You can take one small step today towards it, but it's a step you're going to have to take every day.

2. Determining levels of integrity with employees

When it comes to integrity with employees they know instinctively whether a boss is being honest with them or not.

In addition therefore to determining levels of integrity with customers you will need also to do this with employees.

Employee integrity is only achieved when you treat employees as if they were genuine people with as many needs as yourself. Mutual respect, dignity and genuine equality are the essence of a relationship based on integrity. You will need to recognize and value the unique contribution each person in the team can make.

Initially you will need to come to terms with yourself and your own attitudes towards the people in your team. In this way you will learn that you have nothing to hide; you will believe in yourself. In challenging your own strengths and limitations honestly and humbly you can help yourself overcome previously suppressed weaknesses and learn from unacknowledged mistakes.

You will begin to recognize others' imperfections in yourself and thereby learn to respect them for what they are – having the same potential as yourself for good and bad.

As soon as you have 'genuinely checked yourself out' and gained confidence as a result you will be in an excellent position to double-check with your team the level of integrity in the relationship they have with you. Unless you approach them humbly and are totally open and honest with them (about your thoughts, your hopes, your aims as well as your doubts and concerns) they will not be open and honest with you about their perceived level of integrity in the relationship.

Put simply, you must ask your team about the level of integrity they perceive in the relationship. You can only do this when you've come to terms with yourself and are prepared to learn from your team.

To facilitate the 'asking process' and encourage feedback you will need to create an appropriate climate and forum for people to be open with you. Credible bosses take their teams away for a couple of days to achieve this, often using the help of an external facilitator to provide independent guidance.

Integrity is an essential key for superb team performance, excellent customer service and long-term business success.

You must therefore take this step of determining levels of integrity with customers and employees alike. It might prove incredibly painful, but all you have to do is ask yourself: 'Do I display integrity as a manager?' If you don't know the answer you have a problem. If the answer is 'No', you can immediately start work to develop integrity. Having asked yourself the question and answered it truthfully, double-check the answer with your customers and employees.

Step 6

Resolving conflicts

'The sixth step is to re-examine your principles in an attempt to iron out any conflict within them. This should be done on an ongoing basis.'

Many key management principles are not compatible with one another. Such apparent conflict is enough for many managers to discard principles all together and revert to instinctive behaviour.

For example, openness and honesty do not sit comfortably with caring. Being open when you think badly of an individual can easily shatter that person's inner dignity, cause him or her to lose face. This conflicts with caring which includes preserving face and inner dignity.

Delegation does not always sit comfortably with trust. You just know that a junior, with his or her limited experience will do a job less well than yourself.

When faced with difficult decisions about people, bosses need to be very clear about the underlying principles involved and the extent to which they conflict. In thinking it through, another principle often emerges which helps resolve the conflict. In fact a hierarchy of principles evolves. For example the principle of 'what is best for the individual' might be in conflict with 'what is best for short-term profit', which in turn might be in conflict with 'what is in the long-term interests of all employees'.

Deep-thinking and constructive debate will help resolve such conflicts. It is the lack of such thinking and debate which leads to, for example, short-term profit over-riding many other key

234

principles (such as safety and welfare). Conflicts between the individual and the group are less easy to resolve, albeit as a general principle 'the greater good of the group should prevail while minimizing any individual sacrifice'.

Other conflicts arise for example when one is hesitant about being open and honest with a person you instinctively do not trust. How can you trust a person who manifestly does not subscribe to the same values as you? An instinctive reaction of self-protection and cautious expediency would be preferable in over-riding the principle of openness, honesty and trust. The naïve application of principle is a betrayal of yet another principle.

The skill of those who lead to succeed, therefore, is to identify the underlying principle necessary for any critical decision and behaviour.

An over-riding factor is conscience, and this is dealt with in Step 8. To help you with Step 6, take the most difficult decision you've had to make recently and try to identify the conflicting principles facing you. How did you resolve that conflict? What over-riding principles emerged?

Step 7
Let employees be themselves

'Step 7 is to ensure you let your people be themselves.'

To succeed people must be themselves. Failure comes from striving to be other than yourself. Emulation of the corporate psyche within an individual merely serves to destroy individuality.

The best leaders are those who are themselves, who evolve their own beliefs and values, who express their own feelings and opinions, who develop and grow their own sense of being.

The best leaders are those who, within the overall visionary direction of the organization encourage their people to be themselves, to express their own thoughts, to reveal their own personalities, to develop their own innovative contributions as extensions of themselves.

The worst leaders are those that emulate others, who follow the fashion, who unthinkingly apply other people's rules, who don't think for themselves but adopt the thoughts of others. Such leaders are thoughtless.

The worst leaders are those who attempt to impose the organization's thoughts upon their teams, who attempt to brainwash them with corporate propaganda. They attempt to make their people clones of the system, mere pawns or robots within the organization.

To be successful a key premise is that everyone in the organization must be committed to achieving their own vision of that success.

When a boss attempts to get his or her people to be other than what they want to be tensions will inevitably arise. In reaction to such pressure people become themselves by playing games, pretending to be something different with their bosses than what they really are. Integrity becomes eroded.

Attempts to impose a corporate style, a corporate philosophy, a corporate commitment will fail unless everyone within that organization wants to be corporate as a way of expressing themselves. Such is the pride in working for a reputable company. Everyone wants to be part of the visionary process of achieving corporate success.

It is a fallacy to think that a boss can 'patch' on to his or her people certain sets of beliefs, values, commitments, thoughts and opinions. The patching process is of indoctrination through training, through exhortation and videoed corporate communication.

Successful bosses do not express a corporate message, they express themselves. Successful bosses do not rely on corporate philosophy, they rely on their own philosophy. Similarly they allow their people to evolve their own philosophy, their own beliefs. By a process of healthy debate and argument there will invariably be a tendency towards a convergence and sharing of these beliefs.

In achieving integrity, therefore, open argument is essential. Organizations cannot survive without it. Yet many organizations seek to suppress argument, fearing its consequence as they fear rebellion.

To be yourself you must disagree. Progress is based on constructive disagreement. We will always be disagreeing with one another because we all see things differently, we are all that unique. Healthy disagreement will normally yield unity. As soon as unity has been established there will be further disagreement as further progress is required. Unity is never static. The world moves on and our perceptions of it do too.

To be ourselves we must express our perceptions of the world – of our organization, of our boss – no matter how unpalatable and disagreeable they are. In that way we learn and others do too. In that way we improve.

To be ourselves we must disagree with ourselves, constantly challenging the relationship between our own beliefs, words and actions. Such is integrity and as such we achieve credibility. We can temporarily achieve unity within ourselves – but it is never permanent.

The world moves on tomorrow to bring fresh challenges, even within ourselves.

Those organizations and bosses that suppress disagreement, that simulate permanent agreement among their people are never as successful as those that encourage healthy disagreement and challenge.

The seventh step is to answer two fundamental questions:

1. Am I really myself at work?

2. Do I encourage, as a boss, my people to be themselves?

If the answer is 'yes' to both, just double-check with your team to ensure that you are not inadvertently forcing upon them behaviours alien to them.

If the answer is 'no' sit down with those around you and quietly work out ways in which you and your team can 'free-up' and be yourselves, as opposed to clones of the organization.

Step 8

Check your conscience

'Conscience is undervalued and often neglected in modern-day management. Its application however is vital to the long-term success of an organization. Step 8 is to check your conscience.'

Just as a conscience has a vital role in life it should have a vital role in management and leadership.

Conscience is the cornerstone of integrity. It over-rides faulty logic, impaired principles and defective analysis. It rises above brainpower, competence and capability to point to the right decision when a point of principle is at stake.

In relating to people, whether they be bosses, team members, colleagues, other employees, customers, suppliers, conscience is frequently required. The instinctive answer is not always the best answer, nor is the rational answer. Rationales can be notoriously erroneous. Conscience often dictates that there is a more honest answer, a better answer. It is easy to turn one's head aside and ignore abuse by others. Conscience will dictate that one should confront the issue.

Many managers get trapped in cultures where the play of conscience is not permitted, for example negotiating procedures with trade unions, giving explanations (or rather excuses) to customers, hiding the truth about the organization from the outside world, making decisions that are not in the interests of the community or of the employees.

Incredibly successful leaders allow their consciences to surface, they allow their consciences to influence key decisions when vested interests are in conflict.

Furthermore, they are even prepared to put their jobs on the line on 'issues of conscience'.

Ultimately credibility and respect will only be achieved by those who allow their consciences to guide them. Those who compromise principles and resort to expediency under pressure from others will never succeed in the long term.

Allowing one's conscience to surface and influence direction gives immense strength. By probing deep into one's conscience one discovers a degree of courage which could never be realized by any process of logic.

By putting one's conscience to the fore one can lose everything in the short term but gain everything in the long term. The converse is true. By ignoring one's conscience one can gain everything in the short term but achieve nothing in the long term.

On what issues of conscience are you prepared to stand firm in your organization? If you cannot answer that you are not fit to be a leader. Step 8 is to ask yourself this question and answer it honestly.

Step 9

Ensure consistency

'The key theme of this book is that managerial performance derives primarily from leadership credibility. Credibility is a reflection of integrity in that a leader's behaviours and actions consistently reflect his or her words which in turn are a reflection of his or her beliefs. Having taken the previous eight steps you now need to double-check that what you say is consistent with what you mean and what you actually do.'

In the absence of belief, words and actions will be all over the place; they will become subject to the fleeting winds of organization change and to the fashionable whims of expedient bosses.

To become an incredibly successful boss you must therefore carefully evolve a personal set of beliefs and values which are in fact an embodiment of yourself. Such beliefs and values form the springboard for your behaviours, decisions, actions and words.

In themselves, beliefs and words are meaningless. To acquire meaning they must be converted into action. A belief in 'caring for employees' has no meaning unless there is action to care for employees. Furthermore, any action that is perceived as uncaring will undermine the credibility of the manager who expressed the belief.

While total integrity can rarely be attained (as a consequence of our many imperfections) progress towards it is a realistic possibility day-by-day. It means measuring your words as opposed to using them loosely. It means evaluating decisions and actions in the context of your own beliefs as opposed to reacting to the pressures of others. It means challenging conventional wisdoms and questioning 'the system'. Conventional wisdom and the 'system' is often devoid of real belief and is often no more than a ritualization of highly imperfect historical behaviours within the organization. Conventional systems provide a comfortable framework for the short term only, but these frames become too rigid and restrictive and organizations outgrow them. The risk is that employees and managers are then forced into semi-corrupt behaviours to circumvent the system.

Superbosses pit their beliefs against the rigidity of the organization system. In doing so they progressively evolve a working framework for the achievement of their goals. As such they re-invigorate the organization, continually renewing its systems, continually revitalizing their teams.

The conventional system can never lead to success. At best it limits an organization to limp versions of previous successes. At worst there is total restraint and no success.

Success comes from within. It comes from an evolution of organization systems and culture which embraces the evolving beliefs of its leaders and people. It comes from a consistent application of these beliefs into words, decisions and actions. As such the belief becomes meaningful, its application leading to progress and success. Ideally it is a visionary belief about being the best. Ideally it is a set of beliefs based on principles such as openness, honesty and trust. Ideally it is a belief about the people in the team and the cohesiveness with which they work. Ideally it is a belief in the products and services the organization provides and the consequent excellent level of customer satisfaction. Ideally it is the consistent application of these beliefs that leads to personal integrity and high credibility in the eyes of the world.

So take this penultimate step and ensure that what you actually do today, tomorrow and thereafter is a reflection of what you actually think and say.

Step 10

Finding time to think

'The final step is to find time now and on an ongoing basis to review progress in taking the previous nine steps.'

Integrity and credibility drains away when we do not have time to think. Conversely, integrity and credibility can only be reinforced by significant amounts of thinking time. Without this one is in danger of becoming reactionary, of reverting to unthinking, instinctive behaviour divorced from principle.

To think about what you do is common sense. To think deeply about what you do is less easy. Managers tend to rush around in an increasingly frenetic world; they find that easy. But in doing so they often neglect the essentials of teamwork. If they don't have time to spend with the team they definitely don't have time to think how effective that team is. And if they don't have time to think about teamwork, or people, or you, they certainly won't have time to think about their values, beliefs, principles, vision and many other facets essential to the integrity and credibility required for success in management.

Great leaders are those who have time to think. They find time. They go away for two or three days to think with their team. They think for themselves too. They walk the fields. They take frequent breaks. They shut themselves away and they think. They think about success and failure. They think about management philosophy. They think about their people. They think about their organization.

They think about what they think.

It is not easy to think deeply. It means extracting oneself from all the surface thinking, the reactionary thinking, the distractive thoughts and the automatic thinking that happens on a regular basis. Jumping to conclusions, taking things for granted, failing to question, inability to listen, readiness to be diverted on to another subject are all symptoms of someone who doesn't have time to think.

Thinking deeply means thinking differently. It means challenging oneself. It means starting from the premise that one could be totally wrong, that there could be a totally different light in which to see the problem. It means examining issues from other angles. It means relating your own behaviour to principles. It means questioning and even more questioning. It means humility. It means acquiring an even better understanding of things you thought you understood. It means having the courage to acknowledge your own failings and imperfections.

It means discovering the unpalatable truth about oneself and meeting the challenge of addressing this.

The way to achieve integrity, credibility and success in management is to devote a lot of time by yourself and with your team, thinking through how your actions relate to your words and beliefs.

Such a process is an incredible voyage of discovery!